"I love this book! Julie shares her inspiring journey of learning to hear God's voice, ignore her fears and say *yes* to God's promptings at the store, the mall, the workplace and even online. Julie fills the pages with powerful testimonies as well as great tips on how to listen for God's voice and share His gifts of love in a way that is fun and stress free. *No More No* will inspire your heart with a new level of faith for hearing God's voice and ministering His love and power in everyday living."

—J. Nicole Williamson

Author of five books including *Heaven's Secret of Success*

Founding Director, King's Lantern International

www.KingsLantern.com

"*No More No* not only inspires, but gives practical steps to become free from fear, listen to God's voice and boldly share words and gifts from God's heart. Julie's personal stories prove the joy and adventure found in living totally abandoned to God. Mundane trips to the grocery store become fun opportunities to convey God's love to your world!"

—Brenna Stull

Author and International Speaker

www.BrennaStull.com

"*No More No* helped me reconnect with the truth of who I am in Christ and encouraged me to listen more intently to the Holy Spirit's leading on my mission trips to Papua New Guinea and The Solomon Islands as well as at home. I never want to give in to my fears as a witness for Jesus Christ again!"

—Rick Rupp

International House of Prayer (IHOPKC) Missionary

Director, Topeka House of Prayer

www.RickRupp.com

"There is a time for learning and a time for action. In reading *No More No*, I'm truly convicted that even though I'm a fulltime missionary, I have spent far too much time trying to learn, and not nearly enough time trying to simply do what Jesus did. Julie's numerous (and often humorous) examples of this commitment to say *yes* to Jesus daily have inspired me to go and do likewise!"

—Scott Sullivan
Director of New Initiatives
Frontiers France

"Julie Earl is an amazing Christian leader and someone who walks out what she teaches. As you read *No More No* you will see for yourself the dynamic walk of faith she demonstrates. I highly encourage you to not only read this book, but to invite Julie as a speaker to your next retreat or conference for a life-changing encounter with the Lord."

—Tom Grossman Sr.
Author of *The Praying Church: It Happens Every Day*
Founding Director, Praying Church Institute
www.pcipray.org

"dear julie...i love what you have written. clean and powerful and authentic. i will be glad to support this book. recommend it. just let me know when, where, how. God's hand is on you!   love, ann"

In Memory of Ann Kiemel Anderson

Ann Kiemel Anderson was a best-selling author and highly popular Christian speaker in the 1970's and 80's. Her goal was to change the world with God's love one person at a time—and she did! I never met Ann in person, but her stories inspired me to believe that God's love flowing through me could change my world.

Ann read the first part of *No More No* and her response, in her characteristic lowercase writing, is above. Unfortunately for the world she loved, Ann graduated to heaven on March 1, 2014. Ann is now part of that *"great cloud of witnesses"* (Hebrews 12:1) cheering us on and praying that we, too, will express God's love to our world.

Random Comments

"No More No could completely change how you live your life…it did mine!"

—Barbara S.

"I'm excited to use this book in my own life and as a teaching source to help people hear God's voice and boldly step out and act on it!"

—Mary Ann E.

"I fell in love with this book from the moment I started reading it, and I began having my own encounters with people who needed prayer after the first two chapters!"

—Nancy R.

"At first I thought it might be a book only for superheroes, but it's more like in *The Lego Movie*—it's accessible to the Everyday Guy!"

—Scott S.

"This is a great read for those who want to begin a relationship with God and for those who want their relationship to grow."

—Matt W.

"The encounters Julie shares are excellent examples of how Jesus wants to love and speak through us to reveal His heart."

—Donna P.

"I cried at Julie's intense boldness in the theatre. Wow! Come on, Jesus!"

—Karis J.

No More No

SAY YES TO GOD AND LET HIM SPEAK, WORK AND LOVE THROUGH YOU

JULIE EARL

CAYM
Publishing

McKinney, Texas

Library of Congress Control Number: 2015901058

ISBN: 978-0-9861033-0-8

The author has added personal notes within scriptures using brackets.
Pronouns referring to God have been capitalized out of respect and honor.
Quotes used with permission.

Cover concept by Julie Earl
Cover art and layout by Eric Nishimoto and Shig Katada
Photography by Shig Katada—www.KatadaKreations.com

Visit Julie Earl at: www.CrazyAboutYou.org or www. JulieEarl.com

---

For personal or group Bible studies done in conjunction with *No More No,* look for the *No More No Bible Study Guide* to be released summer 2015.

Table of Contents

Why Read No More No?

For Christians:

As a teenager, I was inspired by the true stories of Ann Kiemel[1] in her book *I'm Out to Change My World*. In her simple, sweet style she shared God's love everywhere she went—at gas stations, on planes, in grocery stores and in her neighborhood. I longed for that same freedom and boldness. I was bursting at the seams, aching to tell people of God's love for them, but hindered by my fears and my continual search for the perfect method or formula. I didn't realize the key to sharing God's love isn't found in formulas, but in listening for God's voice.

No More No shares my journey to hearing God's voice and my discovery that God simply wants us to say *yes* to Him when He asks us to say or do something. We don't have to memorize formulas or specific Bible verses, or plan out conversations ahead of time. We can simply say *yes* to His promptings and allow His words, gifts and love to flow through us.

This book will help you break free from fear and apathy, listen for God's voice and discover the thrill of saying *yes*.

For Seekers:

If you have not yet said *yes* to Jesus, asking Him to forgive you and live inside you, I believe my journey to an intimate relationship with God will allow you to understand more clearly the Father's love for you.

God created you extremely special. No one in the world has ever been, or will ever be, exactly like you with your incredible characteristics, gifts and thoughts. You are a delight to God's heart, and He longs to spend now and eternity walking and talking with you. He wants to fill you with His incredible love, wisdom, strength, comfort and joy. He doesn't promise life will be perfect, but He does promise that you can walk in His perfect love.

For Family and Friends:

No More No will help you finally figure me out! You'll discover how God's love has so thoroughly captured my heart and made me passionate to share that love with my world. Thank you for all your support and kindness. It's a blessing to do life with you!

⸻❦⸻

If you have questions or would like to learn more about God's incredible love for you, please visit my website, sign up for my newsletter and join me on Facebook and Twitter. It would be an honor to hear from you.

God bless you!

Julie

CURRENT ADDRESSES:
www.CrazyAboutYou.org
or www.JulieEarl.com
and
www.facebook.com/CrazyAboutYouMinistries
https://twitter.com/JulieEarlCAYM

For personal or group Bible studies done in conjunction with *No More No*, look for the *No More No Bible Study Guide* to be released summer 2015.

Dark Glass Disclaimer
(Hamster View)

Paul said, *"We see through a glass, darkly"* because there is so much we won't be able to see and know this side of heaven (1 Corinthians 13:12 KJV). I picture each of us in something like a hamster exercise ball that rolls around on the floor. We are only able to see the world from the confines of that little space and where we can roll it. It's not only small and has limited exposure, but it's also been darkened by the filthy lies of Satan.

The good news is that God gives us *"a spirit of wisdom and revelation"* (Ephesians 1:17) and reveals His truths *"precept upon precept; line upon line"* (Isaiah 28:10 KJV) as we pull up our sleeves, rub away Satan's lies, and follow God's leading wherever He takes us.

If you haven't rubbed off the same lies or rolled to the same places I have, please consider my viewpoint with an open heart. Satan wants us to have critical, faultfinding spirits, but the Father wants our spirits to stay tender and teachable because there is still so much He wants to show us of His truth, love and power.

So squeeze into my little exercise ball with me, and let me show you what I've seen and discovered!

For John came neither eating nor drinking, and they say, 'He has a demon.' The Son of Man came eating and drinking, and they say, 'Here is a glutton and a drunkard, a friend of tax collectors and 'sinners'. But wisdom is proved right by her actions.

Matthew 11:18-19

Part 1

Interactions with God

Chapters 1 through 3 share my journey to God and my discovery that He desires to work in and through us to share His gifts with the world when we simply listen for His voice and say *yes*.

Feel Free to Skip the First Two Chapters if:

- You have a firm grasp of God's love and forgiveness
- You are already convinced God is able to speak to you and through you
- You don't want to read my personal stories of discovering God's love, God's voice and God's power

Not everyone will have a desire to know my story and that's perfectly fine! Chapter 3 jumps into how to hear God's voice and say *yes* to His promptings, so feel free to start there.

Chapter 1

God's Talking

❧*In My Socks*❦

It was February 2009—the day before my 42nd birthday. I had been busy home schooling, running various errands and shopping for the weekly groceries.

I had foolishly worn my black, high-heeled boots that were stylish, but not especially comfortable, and now my feet were killing me. As I got into my minivan in the grocery store parking lot, I breathed a sigh of relief. I pulled off my boots and started the van. I wanted to get home quickly to enjoy the early birthday meal my three teenage children and my husband were preparing for me. As I pulled out of the parking lot, I was surprised to see a gentleman sitting by himself in a large, overgrown grassy area across from the grocery store.

The strong thought came out of nowhere. *"Tell him I love him."*

God, is this You talking to me? My feet are killing me, I'm tired and my birthday meal is waiting for me. This wouldn't be Satan, I reasoned. *He'd never tell me to love someone for him. This can't be my flesh—I'm exhausted. This must be You, Father. Okay. If the guy is still there when I get the van turned around, I'll talk to him.*

It only took a few minutes to swing back around, but I quickly realized there was nowhere to park. I knew this was not a busy two-lane road, so I turned on my hazard lights and parked as close to him as possible.

My feet were sore, so I didn't even put on my boots, but just stepped out of the van in my black socks. I decided to grab a bag of Chile-Cheese Fritos® from the back of the van in case the man was hungry. As I headed toward him, trying to watch where I stepped in the tall grass, I called out, "This may sound crazy, but I felt like God wanted me to stop and tell you He loves you."

He stood up and headed toward me. As we neared each other, I realized this was a big guy, especially compared to my 5' 1½" self. But I had perfect confidence that God would protect me since He sent me.

"It's not crazy at all," he said as I finally got close to him. He appeared to be in his mid-forties or early fifties. "I've been working at a gas station for three years dressing up as Uncle Sam and waving to cars as they drove by. I did the job when no one else would no matter how hot or cold. But new management just took over and they cut my hours, so I can't make it financially. I came to the store to buy a sleeping bag because now I have nowhere to live. While I was sitting here waiting for the bus, I asked God if He was there and if He cared."

Wow, God, it really was You speaking to my thoughts! "My name is Julie." I reached out and shook his weather-worn hand.

"My name is Matthew," he said with a big grin.

"God is here, Matthew, and He loves you very much. He cares about everything in your life, and He's going to help you get through this difficult time."

He told me he was a Christian, but not as close to the Lord as he'd like to be. I told him more about God's love for him, and about the local homeless shelter nearby.

"Can I pray for you?" I asked.

"That'd be great! Can we hold hands?"

Thank You, Lord, for allowing me to be Your hands for this dear man.

I took his hands and closed my eyes. "Father, thank You for Matthew. Thank You for reminding him of Your incredible love. He is so special to You. You think about him all the time. Help Matthew through this difficult situation. Give him a job that will meet all his needs. Find a place for him to stay that he can afford. I sense, Lord, that Matthew has been called to a powerful ministry to share Your love with others. Guide him step by step on the rest of his journey. Help him seek You daily and follow Your wisdom and leading. Allow him to feel Your love every moment of every day.

You love him tenderly. Keep his eyes on You alone because You will take care of the rest as he follows You moment by moment. In Jesus' name we pray. Amen."

When I opened my eyes, there were tears running down his cheeks. He looked up and his face was full of joy and hope. God had come and ministered to Matthew's heart as only God can. *Thank You, Father!* I gave Matthew a hug.

"Thank you," he said with a huge smile. "This means so much to me!"

I picked the bag of chips up off the ground where I had set it, and handed it to him. "Let me get something." I ran to the van, grabbed the twenty-dollar bill I had in my purse and handed it to him just as the bus was coming to the bus stop not far from us. I gave him another hug. "God bless you, Matthew. He has great things for you!"

"Thank you again!" He picked up his sleeping bag and headed to the bus, waving and smiling until he disappeared inside. I waved and smiled back.

My heart was bursting with joy as I drove home. *Thank you, Holy Spirit, for allowing me to be Your hands and voice today. That was such fun. What a great birthday gift. I don't think Matthew will ever forget Your love expressed to him through a little gal in her socks. What a sight. I love You!* I felt the Lord laughing and smiling with me as we mused together over the scene that had just played out.

Keep talking to me, Holy Spirit. I'm listening.

⌒⌘⌒

I haven't always been listening. I haven't always known He was talking.

I was born in the small town of Marion, Ohio to a Catholic couple, Dan and Judy Neidig (pronounced "nigh" like in night—"dig"). They had been high school sweethearts, but after eight years of marriage they were in the process of a divorce. In the midst of this heartache, my mother found out she was pregnant with her third child—me. She was overwhelmed and distraught. She didn't want another little one to care for, but the moment the doctor placed me in her arms she fell in love. She now had two sons and a

9

baby girl. She knew somehow we would get through this painful ordeal.

Two-and-a-half years later, God graciously led my mother to a kind, gentle man named Pat O'Hara who was a Certified Public Accountant. Pat had grown up in the Baptist church, but he didn't have a relationship with God. My mother knew marrying a non-Catholic wasn't allowed in the Catholic church, but because of the divorce, she had already been excommunicated from taking the sacraments and going to confession. She didn't have anything else to lose, and she felt Pat was a gift from God, so they were married when I was almost three years old.

Since my new dad was easygoing, we continued to attend the Catholic church as a family. Mom had been taught that being a good person and going to church were the ways to earn favor with God and keep out of hell, so we weren't about to miss.

A NEW CREATION

Four-and-a-half years into their marriage, my mother read a book about the second coming of Christ and realized she wasn't ready if Jesus returned to take believers to heaven. Although she did many good things, she knew her heart wasn't right with God. She had gone to confession her whole life, but had never felt true sorrow for her sin. She had even made up sins as a young person just to have something to say to the priests. But it was as if her spiritual eyes were opened for the first time and she truly believed Jesus was sent to save the world and she needed to be saved. She now understood her sins separated her from God and it broke her heart.

Not realizing she could pray directly to God, she disregarded the church's rules and went to confession in spite of her excommunication. She immediately felt the weight of her sins lift off her shoulders when she cried out to Jesus for forgiveness.

A few days later, a new Christian friend explained that this experience was called being born again. In John 3:3 Jesus said, "*No one can see the kingdom of God unless he is born again.*"

My mother had been born again. She was a new person. Her sins—past, present and future sins—would never be held against her again. They were completely forgiven and she was a new creation. Second Corinthians 5:17 says, "*...if anyone is in Christ, he is a* *new creation; the old has gone, the new has come!"* God now saw my mother as righteous and holy, and the weight of her sins was gone (see 2 Corinthians 5:21).

She instantly noticed changes. She found the Bible to be exciting and wanted to read it every day, and she now saw her actions and attitudes from a different perspective—God's perspective. While reading the Bible and smoking, it dawned on her that smoking was harming her health and wasn't in line with God's love for her body. She immediately quit and never smoked again. She also realized she was dressing in a way that might cause men to struggle with their thoughts, so she dressed more modestly. No one told her these things. It was God's Spirit gently working in her heart.

She no longer had only a head-knowledge of who God is and what He does. She now had a love relationship with Him, and she had more peace and joy than she ever thought possible. I immediately noticed the changes in her and I wanted that same peace, joy and guidance for my life. I was only seven, but I'll never forget the day I knelt by my parents' bed and asked Jesus to forgive me and be in charge of my life. There were no fireworks, but I knew everything was different. God's love filled my heart and I was a new person.

INTRODUCED TO THE HOLY SPIRIT

Less than two weeks later, my parents were invited to a Full Gospel Business Men's Fellowship. At a Bible study connected to that group, they prayed for my mother to be baptized in the Holy Spirit (filled with the power of the Holy Spirit—God's Spirit). She didn't feel any different, but as she was reading the Bible the next day, the word *faith* jumped off the pages. *For heaven's sake,* she thought. *I need to have faith. I have received the baptism of the Holy Spirit, but I just didn't believe it.*

Just as the Holy Spirit did for the disciples in Acts chapter 2, He gave my mother the gift of praying in another language (tongues) to confirm His work in her heart. *"When the day of Pentecost came, they were all together in one place....They saw what seemed to be tongues of fire that separated and came to rest on each of them. All of them were filled with the Holy Spirit and began to speak in other tongues as the Spirit enabled them"* (Acts 2:1-4). One of the words she heard as she prayed in this new language was *Abba*. When she learned that *Abba* is the Hebrew word for *Father*, she was convinced this gift was real.

The evangelical church we began attending taught us many wonderful biblical truths, but unfortunately it didn't teach about the gifts of the Spirit or about God's desire to speak to us. Even though we saw the power of the Holy Spirit discussed throughout the New Testament, we grew very little in this area. We were taught we could ask God to direct us to the right job, the right spouse and the right house to buy, but we weren't taught He was constantly talking to our thoughts and wanting to communicate specifically with us and through us.

As my parents became involved in Bible studies and church, my dad's faith grew until he, too, opened his heart fully to God's love. Our family matured in our walk with the Lord, but it wasn't until I was a teenager that we began to learn more about the gifts of the Spirit and the ways God communicates.

PAPUA NEW GUINEA

My two older brothers, Chris and Dan, were grown and out of the house when my parents, my younger brother, Mike, and I decided to move overseas and work with a Christian mission organization. I was sixteen years old and Mike was eleven. We had been looking at different ministries, but still hadn't found a good fit when we felt God was leading us to put our house on the market. The first family who came to look at the house had just returned from Papua New Guinea.

When they heard why we were selling our house, they told us about a need for an accountant in Madang, Papua New Guinea with Lutheran Shipping. We pulled out the globe and discovered Papua New Guinea shared an island with Irian Jaya, Indonesia. It was located just north of Australia. After a great deal of prayer, we all had a peace about Dad accepting the job. It worked out nicely in the sense that we didn't have to raise financial support and we were still able to share God's love with the precious New Guineans.

When we first arrived, we experienced culture shock. Papua New Guinea (PNG) is a tropical rain forest that is absolutely beautiful with treed mountains and rolling hills. The town where we lived, Madang, was on the water and it reminded me of Hawaii.

But, sadly, in spite of the beauty, most of the people lived in shacks thrown together with scraps of wood. They had cooking fires in the middle of their shacks with a hole in the roof for ventilation.

The house we lived in was much nicer in comparison, but nothing like our home in America. It reminded me of an old double-wide mobile home on stilts, with louvered windows along the outside walls to catch every bit of breeze possible. The house was on the harbor with the water just eighty feet away, so we did get a slight breeze and had a wonderful view.

Fortunately for me, I had been on two summer-long mission trips with Teen Missions International to France and Israel, so I was excited about this new adventure in spite of all the inconveniences and overwhelming poverty. I had wanted to be a missionary since I was a little girl, so this move was an answer to prayer.

Within a month of arriving, we realized my schooling was a problem. There was an international elementary school in Madang for Mike, but since there wasn't a high school for me, I home schooled for the first half of my junior year. We didn't have all the teacher's manuals and the courses weren't self-explanatory enough, so I was really struggling. I also didn't have anyone my age to hang out with. I was helping with the young children at one of the churches, but being a social person, I battled loneliness.

After struggling through the first semester of my junior year, the Lord opened up the doors for me to attend a boarding school in the mountains run by Summer Institute of Linguistics (SIL), a sister of Wycliffe Bible Translators, called Ukarumpa High School. There are over 860 indigenous languages in Papua New Guinea, so a number of Bible translation groups are working in PNG to get the Bible written in as many of these languages as possible. SIL is based in Ukarumpa.

Nestled in the mountains, Ukarumpa has perfect weather during the day and gets cold enough for blankets at night. Being so close to the equator, the weather is basically the same year round. Madang, on the other hand, is extremely hot and humid all year long. The temperature only cools a few degrees in the evenings, which made it hard to sleep since there wasn't any air-conditioning. So did I want to go to boarding school in Ukarumpa with other kids my age *and* have perfect weather? You bet!

I began school after the Christmas break and quickly met the other forty-three students in my class. Most were from the U.S., but there were a number from various countries around the world such as Canada, Australia, New Zealand, England, Germany and Sweden. I quickly fell in love with the other students and even became student body president my senior year because I'm an organizer and wanted to help in any way I could. Most of the students were MKs (Missionary Kids) and had grown up together or been at the school for a number of years. Even though I was a newbie, they kindly welcomed me in.

We had a great time in spite of, or maybe because of, the social limitations of living in such a small community without modern conveniences. We competed in sports with the nationals; shared God's love in nearby villages with songs, skits and Bible lessons; had spiritual camping retreats; performed school plays; and did regular teenage stuff like video parties, skating parties (on a cement floor) and Bible studies with singing and games.

I was able to call my parents weekly, and I saw them every few months when they came up or I went home for a school break.

THE GIFTS OF THE SPIRIT

During one of my breaks, I was home working on my tan in the back yard and listening to a teaching tape by Chuck Smith, the pastor of Calvary Chapel in California. We had been listening to his teachings for several years and had begun to learn more about the gifts of the Spirit. On this particular day, I was listening to a teaching about tongues. He explained that being baptized in the Holy Spirit and receiving the gift to pray in another language (tongues) are both gifts we have to receive by faith, just as we receive our salvation by faith.

I knew that not all Christians believed in praying in tongues. But Paul, who was given tremendous revelations from Jesus and wrote them down in what is a large portion of our New Testament, made it very clear that he needed to pray in tongues. If he needed this gift, even with all those revelations, then I figured I *really* needed it!

Paul explained in 1 Corinthians chapter 14 that praying in tongues is important for our personal encouragement and growth.

He was serious about us receiving this gift, along with the other gifts, as part of the Christian walk.

Paul said:

- *"eagerly desire spiritual gifts"* (verse 1)
- *"anyone who speaks in a tongue does not speak to men but to God"* (verse 2)
- *"He who speaks in a tongue edifies himself"* (verse 4)
- *"I would like every one of you to speak in tongues"* (verse 5)
- *"For if I pray in a tongue, my spirit prays"* (verse 14)
- When you pray in tongues you are *"praising God with your spirit"* (verse 16)
- *"I thank God that I speak in tongues more than all of you."* (verse 18)

Paul said this is one of the gifts we should eagerly desire because when we pray in tongues, in a language we don't know, our spirit is praying directly to God and praising Him. In the process, our spirit is edified and encouraged. Paul was so blessed by this gift that he prayed in tongues more than anyone else, and he wanted everyone to pray in tongues and experience the same blessings.

Jesus, before He returned to heaven, made it clear that He wanted all believers to be baptized in the Holy Spirit and receive every gift the Holy Spirit offers. *"Do not leave Jerusalem, but wait for the gift my Father promised, which you have heard me speak about. For John baptized with water, but in a few days you will be baptized with the Holy Spirit...You will receive power when the Holy Spirit comes on you"* (Acts 1:4-5, 8).

I was convinced. I wanted all Jesus had for me, so I cried out to God:

Father, I love You. Come and fill me with more of Yourself—with more of Your Spirit. I'm only eighteen and just an ordinary girl, but You are such a big God. Be big in me. I want to receive Your Holy Spirit and all the gifts You have for me so that I can share more of Your love and power with the world. I know some people think being filled with Your Spirit and praying in tongues is weird or not even good, but everything You do, Father, is only good, and I'm willing to be weird for You because this world is not really my home. Please give me more of Yourself and more of Your gifts. I open my heart to receive all You have for me. I invite You to fill me with Your Spirit and pray through me in whatever language You choose.

By faith, trusting that God knew what He was talking about, I began speaking whatever non-English words came out...and the strange words came. I immediately knew I wasn't making this language up because it flowed without me thinking about it. Unlike in elementary school when my friend Beth and I would pretend to speak another language on the school bus to try to impress the other kids, this language flowed freely as I opened my mouth by faith and began speaking. I was excited!

In the weeks and months following, every time I prayed in this language I would recognize many of the same words coming out of my mouth. My short memory could never remember something as complex as that, so I knew without a doubt this was God.

Now that I was allowing the Holy Spirit to pray *through* me in another language, my next step was discovering the Holy Spirit wanted to speak *to* me in my own language.

CHRIST FOR THE NATIONS INSTITUTE

A few months before graduating from Ukarumpa High School, a group from Christ for the Nations Institute[2] in Dallas, Texas came to sing, perform skits, and share stories of God's work in their lives. As I listened to the group, I knew God wanted me to attend Christ for the Nations Institute that fall.

After graduation in June of 1985, my parents and brother traveled with me back to Ohio for a several-month break, and then they returned to PNG for one more year. I flew down to Dallas and had another wave of culture shock. I had gone from Small Town USA, to living in a primitive tropical rain forest, to now arriving in one of the larger cities in the world with skyscrapers and large office buildings in abundance. Two guys from my class in Ukarumpa had decided to attend Christ for the Nations Institute as well, so at least I wasn't completely alone.

Christ for the Nations Institute (CFNI) was a big jump in attendance from my high schools in Ohio and PNG, but since I love people, I worked hard to overcome my insecurity and make new friends. I roomed in a two-bedroom apartment with five other young ladies. With six of us using one bathroom and one kitchen, we had our challenges, but we also had fun together.

LISTENING TO GOD'S VOICE FOR OTHERS

CFNI confirmed what I had already been discovering about the gifts of the Spirit—they are available for all believers. Jesus returned to heaven after dying for our sins and rising from the dead, but He didn't leave us alone and helpless. He sent the Holy Spirit, God's Spirit, to fill us with His love and power.

When the Holy Spirit first came to live inside believers during Pentecost, the disciples were filled with power and spoke in other tongues. The people visiting Jerusalem from other countries recognized the different languages the disciples were speaking, and were in awe that the disciples, who were all from Galilee, were declaring the wonders of God in foreign languages.

Some of the people were making fun of the disciples because they apparently looked drunk. They were probably struggling to stand up and feeling fearlessly happy with God's presence so heavily upon them. Peter explained to the people that the disciples weren't drunk, but that this outpouring of the Holy Spirit was the beginning of the *last days* that Joel had prophesied about hundreds of years earlier.

"In the last days, God says, I will pour out my Spirit on all people. Your sons and daughters will prophesy [speak words from God's heart], *your young men will see visions, your old men will dream dreams...I will show wonders...and signs...the sun will be turned to darkness and the moon to blood before the coming of the great and glorious day of the Lord. And everyone who calls on the name of the Lord will be saved"* (Acts 2:17-21). So from the time the Holy Spirit was first poured out at Pentecost in Acts chapter 2, until the sun is darkened, the moon turns to blood and we see that great and glorious day when Jesus returns, we are living in the last days.

What is the promise for those of us living in the last days? God will pour out His Spirit and we will prophesy, see visions, dream dreams, pray in new tongues and operate powerfully in the love and gifts of the Spirit.

I explain the gifts of the Spirit in more detail in Chapter 4. These nine gifts are word of wisdom, word of knowledge, faith, healing, miracles, prophecy, distinguishing of spirits, tongues and interpretation of tongues (see 1 Corinthians 12:7-11).

A word of wisdom, word of knowledge and prophecy are all words God speaks to our thoughts to benefit us or others. A *word of wisdom* is supernatural insight from God to help us or others know how to deal with a particular situation. A *word of knowledge* is information God gives us about someone that we wouldn't know on our own such as a current illness or a past event in their life. A *prophecy* is a brief glimpse into the future, but the word is also used as a general term to mean all words that come from the Holy Spirit.

First Corinthians 2:16 says, *"We have the mind of Christ,"* so if we have His mind, we can hear His thoughts. He speaks to us and through us to express His heart of wisdom and love—encouraging us that He is here and He cares about every detail of our lives. *"But he who prophesies speaks edification and exhortation and comfort to men"* (1 Corinthians 14:3 NKJV).

Prophecy isn't about doom and gloom or criticizing people. Prophecy is about expressing God's love by sharing words of encouragement (edification), gentle urgings or warnings (exhortation) and words of healing (comfort). Our safeguard is that none of these words will go against God's love and none of these words will conflict with the written Word of God—the Bible.

Sadly, some people have been taught that we don't need to hear God's voice or utilize God's gifts because the Bible is all we need. That lie is part of Satan's schemes to keep us from communicating intimately with God, and to keep us from using the powerful tools God gave us to do His will on the earth. I love the Bible and I read it passionately, but God doesn't want us just to read about others who heard His voice and walked in His power in the past. He wants us to hear His voice and walk in His power right now. The same Holy Spirit that lived in them lives in us—and He can't change. He's still powerful and He's still talking to His children.

TESTING IT OUT

One of my first classes at CFNI was on the topic of hearing God's voice. The professor encouraged us to test out the Bible and see if it was true. Would the Holy Spirit speak to our thoughts if we took the time to listen?

We broke up into smaller groups to give it a try. We didn't do a rain dance or beg or plead. We simply asked God to speak to us. Then we took turns going around the circle sharing what we heard. When it was my turn, I stepped out by faith and spoke what came to my thoughts for one of the other young ladies in the group. I can't remember what I said, but it had something to do with her family—something coming up in the near future for them.

A few weeks later she stopped me in the hallway to tell me that what I had spoken about her family had come true. She was excited that God loved her family so much that He would speak through a stranger to confirm what He was about to do in their lives. I was excited that God had used *me*. We both praised God and hugged each other's necks, thanking God for His goodness.

As I continued walking to my next class, I was overwhelmed and in awe.

Wow, God! You are talking.

Chapter Highlights and Application

Born Again: You become born again and a new creation when you simply believe in Jesus and receive Him into your life. Your past, present and future sins will be forgiven and the Holy Spirit, God's Spirit, will live inside you and lovingly lead you through life. If you're not sure you have received Jesus' forgiveness, today is the perfect day. There is no magic formula. Simply believe Jesus is who He says He is—the Son of God come to earth to save us from our sins. Ask Him to forgive your sins, live inside you and be in charge. Scoot on over, out of the driver's seat, and allow Jesus to take the wheel. He's a much better driver because He knows the right speed, where the potholes are and the correct roads to take.

If you do make this life-changing, eternity-changing decision, please find a good Bible to read and other Christians who can help you grow. My website www.CrazyAboutYou.org has resources to help you on your new journey or to answer questions if you are still investigating Christianity. The back of this book has Bonus Materials with Bible verses and information about Becoming a Christian, the Gifts of the Spirit and other helpful topics.

Baptized in the Holy Spirit: The Holy Spirit wants to baptize (soak, immerse) you in Himself. For some, this happens when you become a born again Christian. For others, this happens later when you ask for and receive this baptism by faith. Sometimes it's dramatic and sometimes it's a step of faith as in my mother's story and mine. In any case, we are all encouraged to daily ask for more of the Holy Spirit in our lives. His love, wisdom and power change us and change the world. If you have not experienced this infilling or if you aren't sure you have, simply ask the Holy Spirit to fill you to overflowing. Whether you have fireworks or not, trust that God will give the Holy Spirit to those who ask. Jesus said in Luke 11:13, *"If you then, though you are evil, know how to give good gifts to your children, how much more will your Father in heaven give the Holy Spirit to those who ask Him!"* We have a good Father who wants to fill us with His Spirit.

Tongues: Many people receive a prayer language (the gift of tongues) once they are filled with the Spirit. But this, too, must be received by faith. Ask God for this gift and then speak by faith whatever non-English words come to your lips. It may feel weird at first, but pray in this language for a little while every day as you get ready in the morning, drive to work or do chores around the house. The more you pray in the Spirit—in your prayer language—the more your spirit will be refreshed and encouraged. Your spirit will be praying as it is directed by the Holy Spirit—and He knows what you need.

God's Talking: The Holy Spirit, God's Spirit, speaks to believers' thoughts. When we share those thoughts with others, the Bible calls that prophecy. This will be discussed in more detail in the upcoming chapters, so begin reading what the Bible says in the New Testament about hearing God's voice and prophecy. Ask God to open your spiritual ears to hear His voice. He has so much He wants to tell you.

Chapter 2

We're Listening

My training at Christ for the Nations was the beginning of a lifetime of learning to hear God's voice. It would be many years before it dawned on me to share His loving words everywhere I went, but at least now I was listening.

During my second semester at CFNI, I met Ron Earl, a country boy from the White Mountains of Arizona. He was a student and the leader of a weekly outreach to one of the more spiritually hardened areas in Dallas. The first time I joined his outreach, I was drawn to Ron's zeal for the Lord and the way he fervently worshiped God when we sang together before going out. The group had powerful encounters as we broke up into twos and threes and shared Jesus' love and truth with individuals outside the bars and restaurants. I found myself signing up for that particular outreach pretty regularly, but quickly realized my motives weren't totally pure because I was attracted to the leader.

After several months, one of my roommates suggested I help things along and bake Ron a plate of cookies to test the waters and see if this was more than a friendship. I made one of my favorites at the time, some moist, thick sugar cookies. After I delivered them, I tried one of the extra cookies and realized the baking powder must have been clumpy because when I bit down, I tasted a bitter spot where it hadn't dissolved properly. I laughingly realized this truly was a test to see if he liked me—in spite of the bitter cookies.

Ron's roommate told Ron that a girl was serious if she made cookies for a guy, so he had better take notice. He did take notice, and the cookies, in spite of the bitterness, did the trick. Our friendship quickly developed into a romance and we were engaged within three months.

Ron graduated one semester before me and then worked in the area until I finished my degree. A month later we were married in a small country church in Arizona near Ron's family. My parents and brother Mike were now training with a ministry called Youth With A Mission (YWAM) at their base in Tyler, Texas. They were preparing to join the *Anastasis*, one of YWAM's mercy ships, but they hadn't left yet, so the timing worked out perfectly for a wedding. Other family and friends made the trip out west to make our day a special one.

Ron and I decided to live in Dallas, but six months after we were married, we began attending a church called Vineyard Christian Fellowship in McKinney. It was located forty minutes north of Dallas, so we eventually moved there to be closer to the church.

Vineyard Christian Fellowship had been started by a man named John Wimber in California. John didn't try to put on a show or impress people. He simply would ask the Holy Spirit to come — and He did. John was good at hearing God and shared amazingly detailed words from the Lord for people. He also saw a lot of people healed when he prayed for them.

It was at Vineyard where I learned more about hearing God's voice as I prayed on the ministry team at the end of the services and as I prayed for people in small group Bible studies.

God Loves Talking With Us

One thing I discovered is that God loves talking with us. He loves to hear what's on our hearts and share what's on His. He delights in hanging out with us. We see proof of this in the Garden of Eden. He hung out with Adam and Eve until the day they disobeyed and their sin separated them from intimacy with Him.

Sin estranged them from God because God is completely perfect and sin can't survive in the fullness of His presence. This concept is easier to grasp by thinking about light. When a light is turned on in a dark room, the darkness ceases to exist. Light now pervades the room. God is all light and all that is perfect and good. First John 1:5 says, *"God is light; in Him there is no darkness at all."* When He enters a "room" all that is darkness ceases to exist. The darkness is swallowed up by the light. The darkness is destroyed. It is gone.

After Adam and Eve sinned, they immediately hid when God came close because they had stepped out of God's light into darkness. Imagine the depths of their despair when they disobeyed God and bit down on that piece of fruit. They lost everything that mattered—their innocence and God's friendship. They lost the amazing intimacy with God they had been created for in the first place. They could no longer walk with Him in the Garden in the cool of the day and enjoy His delight and pleasure. Their shame engulfed them like a sinister, dark cloud of death. Their purity was lost and Satan roared with laughter for having alienated mankind from the God who loved them perfectly and passionately.

Many years later, at just the right time, Jesus came to make a way for that relationship to be restored (see Romans 5:6-19). Because Jesus is God in the flesh—fully God and fully man, and without sin—He was the perfect and final sacrifice for sin. He took the punishment for all sin on Himself. There was no longer a need for animal sacrifices to push back the sins of the people because the payment for sin was paid in full by Jesus. He laid down His life to be the bridge leading us back to the relationship with God that was lost in the Garden.

If we choose to receive Jesus' forgiveness, we have access to a relationship with God that's even greater than evening walks in the Garden. We have the privilege of God's Spirit living within us, and we are able to communicate spirit to Spirit—our spirit to God's Spirit—in constant, unbroken communion.

God Communicates in a Variety of Ways

The beauty of this unbroken communion is that God's Spirit, the Holy Spirit, loves to communicate with us in a variety of ways. He's not limited like we are. He's God! He communicates with perfect wisdom and creativity.

Knowing we aren't always the best at listening, He has utilized an assortment of methods through the years to get His point across. He thundered from the mountains, and He whispered in a still, small voice. He stopped a prophet from cursing the Israelites by making a donkey talk, and He redirected another prophet with a storm and His personal "submarine" in the form of a big fish. He talked from a burning bush, and He spoke through prophets who did strange things to get people's attention. He spoke through dreams and visions, and He led the wise men to Jesus with a star.

God still communicates through obvious methods. He graciously gives us our own *big fish* experiences to redirect our path, and He speaks through dreams, visions, His audible voice, the Bible and other teachers. All of these are wonderful and amazing ways to hear from the Lord, but we must be careful to listen and watch for the less obvious and more subtle ways God speaks to our spirits— the ones we have to be watching and listening for with the eyes and ears of our hearts (see Ephesians 1:18). Let's look at four subtle yet supernatural ways the Holy Spirit communicates through thoughts and promptings, peace or uneasiness, pictures in our mind's eye and pain in our body.

THOUGHTS AND PROMPTINGS

When Jesus came to earth, He operated through the power of the Holy Spirit (God's Spirit) and listened for the thoughts and promptings of the Holy Spirit. He did this to show us what we can accomplish when we live our lives through the power of the Holy Spirit and constantly listen to His thoughts and promptings. Jesus chose to be completely dependent on the Spirit's voice and leading in order to be our example. He made it clear that we, too, are meant to walk in the power of the Holy Spirit and do even greater things than He did during His short time on the earth.

The key to walking in this power is staying in tune with God's voice. Jesus and the Father were in constant communication with one another, but even though they spoke continually, the Father rarely spoke audibly. Instead, they communicated through their thoughts and promptings. One of the few times the Father did speak audibly in John 12:27-30, Jesus made it clear He didn't need an audible voice to hear the Father. He told the people, *"This voice was for your benefit, not mine"* (verse 30). Jesus didn't need an audible voice because the Father was continually speaking to Jesus' mind and heart in the same way He continually speaks to ours.

Most of the stories* in this book are a result of God speaking to

26

my thoughts and prompting me to share things with people, so you'll see numerous examples of me listening to those promptings and taking risks. But it is just as amazing that God's Spirit is able to speak to our thoughts for all the decisions we need to make in our lives—both large and small.

*Note: There is an Index of Stories in the back of the book for easy reference.

Listening for Marriage

Deciding who to marry is a perfect example of listening for God's thoughts and promptings for big decisions. Ron and I had some concerns about getting married, so we each asked the Lord for wisdom. We were from very different backgrounds. While I grew up in a neighborhood on an acre of land with a garden, I was still mostly a city girl who liked to dress in style, go to the mall, play volleyball, run track and sing solos in church.

Ron grew up in the sticks on forty acres. He wore white T-shirts and jeans, hated shopping, and loved baseball, the outdoors, hunting and playing the guitar. When we took the personality test in the counselor's office, we saw that we were both leaders, which is tough in a marriage. I was a leader who loved to party and have fun. He was a leader who preferred to be alone. The counselor told us it would work, but it would be hard. In the end, we both felt the Lord giving us the *yes* to marry, so we trusted God and made the plunge. Knowing God led us together was a great help and comfort during the years when we experienced tremendous conflict and challenges in our relationship.

In the midst of some of those marriage challenges, I remembered that as a teenager I had read Joni Eareckson's[3] book called *Joni*. In the book she told the story of her diving accident that snapped her spine and left her quadriplegic. Instead of staying bitter, she turned to God and allowed her tragedy to make her more like Jesus. God used Joni powerfully as she learned to draw beautiful artwork with a pencil or paintbrush in her mouth, and as she counseled and spoke with many who were hurting. She began a ministry called Joni and Friends, and has helped countless people deal with handicaps and severe trials, and overcome depression and hopelessness through God's love.

When I read her book, I asked the Lord to do whatever it'd take to make me more like Jesus, and I imagined a wheelchair or blindness. (This was before I realized it was Satan, not God, out to steal and destroy through tragedies, injuries and disease.) Rather than attacking my health, though, Satan attacked my husband's. Shortly before Ron and I were married, Ron developed a noncancerous pituitary tumor that created havoc with his body and emotions.

Back in the early years when the emotions were most intense and I was often in tears, I had a choice to make. Would I become *bitter* or would I allow God to use this to make me *better*—to make me more like Jesus? The Holy Spirit sweetly wrapped His loving arms around me and helped me gradually wrap my arms around my pain. He helped me gratefully embrace the pain and allow it to burn away my own ugly, sinful flesh—my griping and self-pity; my anger and resentment; my pride and self-centeredness; my controlling spirit and other junk that surfaced in the midst of the conflict.

I clung to 1 Peter 3:9 and quoted it almost daily to myself: *"Do not repay evil with evil or insult with insult, but with blessing, because to this you were called so that you may inherit a blessing."* Learning to follow that wisdom was a long, excruciating process. Some days I did well at blessing and loving my husband, and other days I failed miserably. But the more I fell in love with Jesus, the easier it became to love Ron. The more I chose to bless Ron with kind words and loving actions rather than negative words or a cold indifference, the more my heart changed. It took many years with three steps forward and two steps back (or three or four steps back), but eventually our hearts softened. We both became more loving, patient and thoughtful.

We still aren't perfect, and Ron still has to battle the effects of the tumor with supplements and diet. But the more we allow God's loving words and actions to flow through us, the more our uglies are washed away by His love.

I am truly grateful for my amazing husband and how he has chosen to love and provide for us no matter how emotionally and physically challenging his life has been under this attack. We know God wants Ron healed and we believe one day soon the devil's lies telling us Ron can't be healed will be broken off our minds and hearts, and he will be healed.

I agree with the saying "Where God guides...He provides." God led us to marry each other knowing all that we would face, and He provided the strength, comfort and grace to go through the refining fires and come out more pure because of them.

PEACE OR UNEASINESS

Another subtle way the Holy Spirit communicates is by giving us peace or uneasiness in situations or circumstances. Jesus made it possible for us to have peace with God. Romans 5:1 says, *"Since we have been justified through faith, we have peace with God through our Lord Jesus Christ."* When we receive Jesus' forgiveness and submit our lives to God, we are no longer enemies of God, opposed to His wisdom and truth. We are at peace with Him.

God is referred to as the God of peace many times throughout the Bible. When we invite the Holy Spirit to come into our lives, His peace floods every part of us. Philippians 4:7 says, *"And the peace of God, which transcends all understanding, will guard your hearts and your minds in Christ Jesus."* We no longer have to worry or be stressed in any way because we can trust God to take care of us as we walk in His wisdom. Our hearts and minds are guarded by God's peace. It's important, then, that we stay in that peace. If we are seeking God for direction on whether to accept a job offer, which house to buy or about sharing God's love with someone, we must act according to which decision gives us peace and a comfortable feeling.

❧Flagged Down by Angels❧

A great example of following God's peace happened while I was driving back home from the airport. I saw a gentleman standing by his car on an entrance ramp to I-635, one of Dallas's largest and busiest highways. The thought quickly came, *"Help him."* I had to check my peace. I had never stopped to help a man on the side of the road because of obvious safety issues. It was daytime and a lot of traffic was driving by so it looked safe in that regard. I immediately felt a tremendous flood of God's peace fill my mind, so I pulled over behind his car. When I got out of my van and walked toward the man, I saw that he towered over me, but I knew my angels were far bigger and God was leading me.

As it turned out, the man was a Christian. Psalm 91:11 came to mind: *"For he will command his angels concerning you to guard you in all your ways."* This man's angels must have flagged down my angels to stop and help. I envisioned in my mind's eye our angels giving each other high-fives and laughing together—and it made me chuckle. I was able to take the man to get the tool he needed to remove his tire and put on the spare. He said he had been stranded quite a while, but other people who passed were too afraid to stop and help a stranger. He understood their concerns, but he was extremely grateful I had stopped. When he asked how he could repay me, I smiled and patted him on the arm, "God sent me to love you for Him. It was my pleasure. You are an amazing man of God, so just keep doing what I'm sure you're already doing—listening for the Lord's leading and sharing His love with your world!"

It was knowing God's peace and paying attention to His peace that enabled me to help this man in crisis.

⋄

There have been other times when I've wanted to share God's love with someone, but the Holy Spirit gave me an unsettled feeling—an icky, unsure or negative emotion. The peace wasn't there. Perhaps God had somewhere else He needed me or that person to be. Perhaps the person was closed to God's love and the best thing I could do was pray silently for them. Perhaps it would have been unsafe. God knows all the details, so when we get that yucky feeling and a lack of peace, we need to *not* do the thing we were considering.

It is important, though, to realize that Satan's demonic forces (the fallen angels), will shoot fearful thoughts at you every time you feel led to love someone for God. Fear is not from God and it isn't how He communicates. God communicates with a lack of peace. You need to recognize the difference so fear doesn't stop you from doing what the Holy Spirit is guiding you to do.

❧ Yellow Shirt ❧

This is making me laugh, so I have to share it. I have a personal goal for completing the writing of this chapter, so I've been putting off the weekly grocery shopping the past several days in order to write and pray. This morning I figured I could stretch the food one more day and go shopping tomorrow so that I could keep plugging away with my writing. But a few minutes ago, after finishing the previous paragraph, I felt a strong uneasiness in my spirit about *not* going to the store today. I began telling myself all the reasons why tomorrow would be better, but the uneasiness stayed. I'm not sure if this is because my family will be blessed by more food in the house or because I have someone to meet with while I'm there, but I'll let you know when I return....

I'm back.

While I was getting ready to leave the house, I had the thought that I would be talking with a lady in a yellow shirt at the store. The word *relationship* and the name *Sheila* also came to mind. I wasn't sure if these were all tied together, so I asked the Lord to lead me. I picked up my Aunt Patricia from her apartment so she could shop with me, and we headed to the store.

Just inside the doors, there was an older lady and her teenage granddaughter sitting with their groceries and waiting to be picked up. They caught my eye, so I prayed, asking God to bless them because the grandmother looked sad and worn out. I felt impressed to love them for the Lord, so I pushed my cart their direction.

"Hi," I said with a big smile. "I feel like the Lord wants to remind you how special you are to Him. God loves you very much."

The grandmother at first looked confused, but as it dawned on her what I was saying, her eyes lit up and her countenance changed. "We know God," she said, now smiling. "He has made such a difference in our lives!" We chatted about His goodness for a few minutes, and the grandmother looked as if the weight of worry and depression had lifted off her shoulders from this short interchange. I didn't have anything profound to say, but God's love expressed through me, a stranger, profoundly touched her heart. I didn't think to ask if her name was Sheila.

I continued into the store walking toward the return department to take back a few items. As I passed by the bank inside the store, one of the bank employees, a middle-aged lady, was standing in front of the bank trying to encourage people to become customers. You'll never guess what color shirt she and the other bank employees were all wearing today. Yes. Not only yellow, but bright yellow. The lady also had a nametag. Her name *wasn't* Sheila. I began talking with her—a few sentences of banking chit-chat and then about the Lord.

"Before I came to the store today, I felt like God wanted me to talk with someone in a yellow shirt, and it appears you're the person He wants to love," I said. "You delight God's heart. He really loves you." I wasn't getting any specific thoughts about her needs so I asked, "Is there anything I can pray about for you?"

"You can pray I find a husband. A good one!" she laughed.

"That's interesting, because when I got the words *yellow shirt* I also got the word *relationship*." I could tell her interest was piqued. I kept my eyes opened, but placed my hand on her shoulder and prayed, "Lord, bless this dear lady with the man you have for her."

"God's got a godly man for you because He loves you," I said. "Are you in a place where you're able to soak God's love for you?"

"I used to go to church, but the church I attended always seemed so negative. I do listen to encouraging preachers on TV."

I told her about the great teachings and books coming out of Bethel Church in Redding, California by Bill Johnson[4] and other members of their staff, and how they have a good grasp of God's love and delight in His children. I wrote down the information, also giving her my contact information in case she ever wanted to chat or join me at my church. She didn't have any customers the four or five minutes we spoke, and just as we finished talking, people began walking up. "God bless you. I'll let you get back to work. Don't forget how special you are," I said.

"Thank you," she said with a smile.

During the rest of my shopping trip, I was feeling emotionally whacked-out due to hormones and parental challenges, so I just prayed for people I passed. I said kind words and smiled whenever I could, but I didn't feel any urges to talk with anyone else like I usually do. The Holy Spirit is thoughtful and He understands we are human and have times we need to step back.

So my uneasiness about *not* going shopping today got me out of the house to bless my aunt with a trip to the store, bless my family with more food and remind three people how much God loves them and that He would send a stranger to reach out to them with a few kind words. It's important to stay in God's peace.

PICTURES IN OUR MIND'S EYE

A number of years ago I began to get pictures in my mind's eye when I would pray for people. I knew it had to be the Holy Spirit giving me these pictures because I'm not a visual person like an artist or a decorator. I can't envision amazing drawings or decorating schemes. I'm a stick-figure person when it comes to drawing, and I need photos to look at when it comes to decorating.

The pictures I get are like rough sketches. One way to describe them would be to have you close your eyes and picture the furniture in your living room. Your picture may be similar to how I see the pictures when they appear in my mind's eye. I don't see many details or colors unless they are significant to the meaning. I rarely see a person's face, but I immediately know who they are. I'll usually see a picture and then start to talk about it as I keep praying or talking to the person. Oftentimes the picture will be more like a movie where activity is happening as I speak. When I share the picture, the meaning follows. I can have my eyes opened or closed, although it's sometimes easier to focus if they're closed.

ᖰ Back in the Game ᖰ

The Lord gave me a number of pictures one evening while I was at a prayer and worship meeting in a friend's home. We were worshiping in song and praying for each other as we felt prompted by the Lord. At one point I walked over to a young woman I had never met, introduced myself, and asked if I could pray for her. As I asked the Holy Spirit what He had to say, I saw a picture of her on a soccer field in a soccer uniform, but I sensed she wasn't a soccer player. I felt God was moving her forward to do mighty things for Him, but there had been opposition. In my mind's eye I could see the opposing team was comprised of Satan and his demons. I saw a demon running toward her, and just as he was about to kick the ball away from her, I saw two angels grab her, one under each arm, and lift her up and over the demon. The angels kept hold of her arms and lifted her over every opponent, allowing her to keep control of the ball until she reached the goal and made the shot. Jesus was the goal and God was promising her victory as she stepped out by faith and ran in His strength.

After sharing these and other details, I prayed for her and then asked what the Lord had been doing in her life. She told me she had been ministering overseas for several years and had gotten burnt out. She hadn't been doing anything to help others spiritually for quite some time, but the Lord had encouraged her just last week that it was time to "get back in the game." How fun that God directed me to the picture that matched exactly the phrase He had used with her.

⌒⌘⌒

I don't have pictures every time I pray or talk with people, but I try to look for them in case the Holy Spirit is giving me one. The more I look, the more I see them. Like I said, it isn't a full-blown, technicolor movie screen, but a simple sketch that I have to focus in on. I have to look for the picture and then begin sharing by faith no matter how faintly I see it. God honors that faith and continues to reveal more after I begin to speak. I believe God wants to share these pictures, or visions, with all of His children, because as the saying goes, "A picture is worth a thousand words." A picture is often easier to remember, so it has the potential to encourage the person longer. God used visuals throughout the Bible, so it makes sense God would still be into using visuals to help us grasp truth.

PAIN IN THE BODY

There may be times when you'll feel temporary pain in different parts of your body to indicate where someone needs prayer in their own body. This is an easy form of communication from the Holy Spirit, but you'll miss it if you don't pay attention. When you're around other people be aware of your own body. If you feel a pain you've never felt before, find out if someone has some type of pain or injury at that same spot in their own body. If they do, ask to pray for them and believe God for the healing He promised.

Listen Expectantly

Whether God speaks to your thoughts, gives promptings, gives you peace or uneasiness, shows you pictures in your mind's eye, allows you to feel a person's pain or uses other methods, the point is that God is always communicating and He wants you to listen and watch for what He is saying and doing. He wants you to listen expectantly with the faith of a beloved child knowing that your Father, your Daddy, loves to share His heart with you.

Chapter Highlights and Application

Sin and God Don't Mix: God is complete perfection and sin can't survive in the fullness of His presence. You can't live with God, either on earth or in heaven, with your sin—even the smallest sin. If you die before asking Jesus to forgive you and be Lord of your life, then you will spend eternity apart from God in hell. That's why Jesus was beaten beyond recognition and killed on a cross—to pay for your sins. He took the punishment you deserve. He offers forgiveness for your sins as a gift, and if you receive that gift, your sins will no longer be counted against you. You will be righteous and holy in God's sight. God loves you beyond your wildest imagination and wants to fill you with Himself—with His love and inexpressible joy.

God Speaks to Our Minds and Hearts: As a believer, it is important that you listen and look for the thoughts, promptings and pictures the Holy Spirit places in your mind, and the peace He places in your heart. God longs to speak to you and through you wherever you go, but you have to be listening. Make it a point in the next few days to begin listening for God's thoughts and look for pictures in your mind's eye for yourself and others—at home, work, school or the store. Even if you aren't ready to share those thoughts, write them down and check with several other Christians to see if they sound like God's voice. Practice listening. Trust that you can hear from God. He loves talking with His children. He loves talking with you!

Chapter 3

Yes, Lord!

Imagine yourself soaked with sweat, gasping for breath, and forcing one last burst of speed as you push yourself in the final minutes of your run. The timer beeps and you reduce the pace of the treadmill as you catch your breath and look around to see who else drug themselves to the gym this early in the morning. You notice a middle-aged woman sitting near the free-weights, mopping her forehead with a towel. All of a sudden the thought comes: *"She's hurting. Express My love."*

If being at a gym is too much of a stretch for your imagination, picture yourself at your favorite coffee shop. You just sat down with a delicious coffee blend and a whole-grain muffin when the young man sitting at the table next to yours catches your eye. He is perusing the newspaper as he sips his coffee, and the Holy Spirit urges you, *"Pray with him."*

If either of these scenarios strikes fear in your heart, then you're not alone. If your first reaction was, "Here?" or "I don't think so," then you're still not alone. Unfortunately, saying *yes* to God isn't as easy as it sounds. It doesn't come naturally. Relinquishing control and saying *yes* instead of *no* is a battle we are engaged in at different levels our whole lives as we learn to trust God with each new challenge or situation.

The battle begins at birth. A baby isn't born thinking, *I trust God and the parents He gave me, so I want to do everything they ask.* On the contrary, once the little guy can talk, his lack of trust shows up in his choice of a favorite word—*no.* He uses it regularly because he's convinced he knows better than everyone else what's best for him.

"No, I don't want to eat my vegetables." "No, I don't want to take a nap." "No, I don't want to be nice to my sister."

We have been blessed with three wonderful children, but they were no exception to this rule. They were convinced they knew better than us in many areas. They each had to go through the often painful journey of learning to trust and say *yes* to authority, and ultimately *yes* to God.

Feel free to skip these stories if you'd like. They emphasize my point, but their main purpose is to give you a closer glimpse into our lives. Richelle, Dane and Sierra graciously gave me permission to give you a peek into their childhood.

RICHELLE'S JOURNEY

When Richelle was born, we were in awe of God's handiwork. She was our beautiful baby girl. Unfortunately, she had colic and sleep issues, but after we survived the sleepless months and the excessive fussiness, Richelle ended up being a pretty laid-back, obedient little girl. If I asked her to do something, like clean up her toys, she would usually do it. If I asked her not to do something, like touch the pretty ornaments on the Christmas tree, she usually wouldn't do it. She did get disciplined numerous times for fighting with her brother as they both got older, but for the most part, she obeyed and followed the rules.

Her lack of trust didn't show up as much in her behavior as it did in her attitude. She was born with a sensitive nature, but in her immaturity, that sensitivity was focused on *her* comfort and *her* happiness. Any time those were threatened, she let us know about it through whining or complaining. To help with this issue, I made the rule that the kids had to put their nose on the wall for three minutes every time they whined. Richelle spent quite a bit of face-to-face time with the living room wall until she learned to trust her parents and trust God. Rather than whining or complaining when things weren't going the way she liked, she learned to talk nicely about it with us or simply pray and ask God to work out the details. Her focus turned from her comfort and happiness, to blessing others and pleasing the Lord with a grateful heart. Now, as an adult, Richelle uses her sensitivity to sweetly minister God's love and tenderness to others. She supports a Compassion child from Africa, encourages her clients at the salon, and pushes past her quiet temperament to express God's love to her world.

She and her husband, Luke, had their own baby, Ryder, in 2013, and Richelle and Luke are both terrific parents. Richelle is able to tenderly care for and love her little guy, sacrificing sleep, time and money without complaining, because she learned as a young person to say *yes* to God, trusting His wisdom no matter how difficult the challenge. Her *yes* to God, displayed in self-sacrifice, is now blessing the next generation, our first grandchild, and we couldn't be more proud of her.

DANE'S JOURNEY

Dane was born two-and-a-half years after Richelle and he rarely whined or complained, but he didn't have any qualms about doing his own thing. He was a cutie and we enjoyed him in numerous ways. But the majority of my job as his mom, even before he turned two, was summed up in three words:

Spank—Hug—Repeat.

When he was old enough to climb, Richelle *kindly* taught him how to crawl out of his crib. Since that posed a safety problem during his escapes, we quickly bought him a regular bed. The first night in his big-boy bed, we had our usual nighttime routine. He and I talked and prayed, and I gave him a hug and a kiss. I said goodnight and explained clearly that he needed to stay in bed and not get up. Within minutes he came walking into the living room, innocently smiling and enjoying his newfound freedom. I walked him back to his room explaining that he had disobeyed Mommy. I spanked him, told him I loved him, gave him a hug and tucked him back in bed with clear instructions to stay.

In less than three minutes he came out again and I repeated the whole scenario. After he got up the third time, I decided to park my body outside his bedroom door. I grabbed Dr. James Dobson's book *The Strong-Willed Child*[5] and sat on the floor desperately scouring the pages yet again for some miracle cure for disobedience. Dr. Dobson simply said to keep at it. Keep disciplining with love and patience, and don't let the child win.

So I posted myself as guard outside Dane's door, taking him back into his room after each escape. The Spank—Hug—Repeat routine lasted for over an hour. After the twelfth spanking, I was convinced Dr. Dobson was lying. Perseverance hadn't paid off.

The one positive of keeping vigil by Dane's door was that I noticed his doorknob was on backward. My parents, who were now off the ship and living near us in McKinney, had sweetly helped us repaint. All the other doors were correct, but my mom accidentally put Dane's knob back on with the lock on the outside of his door. So after the twelfth time, I told Dane I was going to lock his door and I would unlock it when he chose to obey and stay in bed.

I hoped this would do the trick, but twenty minutes later I heard a loud thud in his room. I went running in and there was Dane looking scared and shocked standing in front of his four-and-a-half foot red dresser that was precariously leaning forward. He had opened all the drawers until it tipped from the weight. Fortunately, the drawers kept it from falling on top of him, but it clearly shook him up. He wasn't the only one shook up. We had yet another talk about the importance of trusting and obeying authority. I gave him a spanking for disobeying, and put him in bed with a hug and an "I love you." This time he *did* stay in bed, and within a few days, he stopped getting up.

We had many of these battles. It was exhausting and discouraging. I couldn't understand why consistent discipline wasn't working, but I was determined to hang in there. I taped Proverbs 29:17 on the fridge and looked at it several times a day for encouragement. *"Discipline your son, and he will give you peace; he will bring delight to your soul."*

Shortly after Dane turned four, we finally had that peace. His stubborn heart submitted to our authority and his constant *no* turned to a *yes*. He began to obey the majority of the time, and we were thrilled. Persistence *had* paid off.

Proverbs 29:17 was right. Dane truly has been a delight. He looks for ways to love intentionally, and his sweet, fun-loving personality keeps us all chuckling and wondering what crazy thing he'll say or do next. He constantly says *yes* to the Holy Spirit, praying with people for healing and sharing encouraging prophetic words of love at college, on the job and wherever he goes.

And, thanks to Dane, if I write a book on parenting I know just what I'll call it—*Dr. Dobson Wasn't Lying.*

SIERRA'S JOURNEY

Little did we know that Dane's disobedience was merely a mild warm-up for some serious parenting challenges to come. When Richelle was fourteen and Dane was eleven-and-a-half, we adopted my nine-year-old second cousin. She came to us as Nichole, but she agreed that a new home and a new lifestyle deserved a new name and signified a fresh start, so she and I picked the name Sierra.

Sierra had a sweet openness and she loved calling us Mom and Dad and sitting on our laps. But due to a number of issues, she didn't respect or trust authority—ours or God's. She didn't believe that we knew better than her, so she rarely did what we asked. She knew to obey in front of us, but as soon as we left the room, she immediately did what she wanted. For over seven years we dealt with almost constant disobedience, lying, stealing and deception. Even though we disciplined Sierra every time she disobeyed, she continued relentlessly.

We tried various counselors and strategies, but nothing seemed to help. Sierra was reading her Bible each morning like the rest of us (at least she was supposed to be). She memorized verses, went to church and heard moving pleas from me that would make grown men in maximum security repent...but none of this seemed to penetrate her heart and mind.

Needless to say, Sierra's continual disregard for rules and authority brought up a lot of frustration and anger in the rest of us. Our family had to learn a whole new level of forgiveness and unconditional love. I thought I had dealt with the worst of my sinful nature during the early marriage years, but I quickly realized my flesh was not yet dead—not even close. Many a night I would lay in bed crying out to God to forgive my anger and irritation, begging for more grace and love.

It was a painful and slow process, but we gradually allowed God to replace our irritation with patience, our criticism with encouragement and our anger with love. We learned to speak God's truth about Sierra—that she is a princess, funny, smart, talented, beautiful, precious and called to do mighty things for God and for others. We saw firsthand that *"Death and life are in the power of the tongue"* (Proverbs 18:21 NKJV). We weren't perfect in our efforts, but even so, we saw God's loving words of truth spoken over Sierra bring new life to her spirit. Her heart gradually softened, and not surprisingly, ours did as well. As we looked at Sierra through God's eyes, we couldn't help but love her more. And the more we loved her, the more her softening heart opened to God's love and ours.

When Sierra was sixteen, the Lord graciously led us to an amazing youth group where the leadership's passionate love for Jesus and powerful messages further touched Sierra's heart. She heard from someone other than her family that God loves her beyond measure and she can trust Him completely. Once she graduated high school and massage therapy, she joined the church's Bible Internship program, and her heart softened further.

Unfortunately, when Sierra moved out on her own, Satan came at her full force with his lies and attacks. But we know our beloved daughter is the apple of God's eye and is destined for greatness. We can't wait to see her step into the amazing life God has planned for her. Her life will inspire many to say *yes* to God's love and wisdom.

My "Yes, Lord!" Moment

Since our Heavenly Father is perfect in love and wisdom it should be easy to say *yes* when He prompts us to do something, right? Why was it, then, that our hearts began to race when I spoke about the scenarios at the gym and the coffee shop?

To put it simply: We don't fully trust our Father.

Satan tells us we'll look stupid, say the wrong thing or ruin our reputation, so we trust his lies rather than the Father's love—and we remain silent.

During the summer of 2011 I faced the fact that I didn't fully trust my Father. When the Holy Spirit would urge me to share His love, I would only say *yes* when I could do it comfortably and easily. I might tell a family member, friend or cashier something neat I heard at church or something powerful God was doing in my life. I might share God's love with the person sitting beside me on the plane. I might even occasionally (very occasionally) stop and talk with random people as the Holy Spirit gave me a word of knowledge or word of love for them (like with Matthew in the first chapter). I was pretty bold, but I was still saying *no* far more than I was saying *yes*. I was being led by Satan's lies rather than God's love.

The ridiculousness of what I was doing finally sunk in. I was saying *no* to the King of Kings, the Lord of Lords, the Creator of the Universe, the One who knows everything and the One who loves me passionately and perfectly. I was acting like a two year old and telling my Father I knew better than Him. I fell to my knees:

I'm so sorry, Father. I've been foolish.
I won't say *no* to Your promptings any longer.
From this day forward I choose to say, "No more no!"
    When You ask me to go, I'll go.
    When You ask me to love, I'll love.
    When You ask me to speak, I'll speak.
    When You ask me to pray, I'll pray.

No matter how scared, stupid or inadequate I feel,
I choose to say, "Yes, Lord!"
    Your heart's desire is to love me
    and love the world through me.
Allow me to be Your hands, Your feet and Your voice.
May Your will be done in my life no matter the cost.
    I love You and I will trust you completely.

That simple prayer changed the course of my life. I went from sharing God's loving words with two or three people each week, to two or three people—or more—almost every time I left my house.

GPS—God's Parcel Service

A number of times in the past I had made similar commitments to talk about Jesus everywhere I went, but I quickly fizzled out when the formulas I used didn't work with the people I met or I couldn't figure out what to say in each situation. I became stressed-out because I felt like the pressure was on me to come up with the perfect thing to say to touch people's hearts.

Fortunately, God had begun explaining His business—God's Parcel Service—more clearly to me. I had worked the business incorrectly in the past and was doing a job I was never asked to do. I had been trying to figure out what people needed from God and then endeavoring, often unsuccessfully, to create packages to give them. God's Spirit living in me, the Holy Spirit, lovingly made it clear that He was the only manufacturer in the business and that I was not to step foot in manufacturing ever again. I was delivery only!

God's Parcel Service (GPS) is like the United Parcel Service (UPS) in that the employees simply pick up the packages and deliver them. When you say, *Yes, Lord,* you are signing up as an employee of GPS. The main job description of a GPS employee is to get the packages from God and pass them out. This takes all the stress and pressure off of you, the employee, and makes the job much easier. You aren't responsible for the packages—just the delivery. You simply listen and watch expectantly for what the Holy Spirit is saying and doing, and then share the gifts of love He desires to give through you.

As a GPS delivery person, you're basically along for the ride. You may be sitting in the driver's seat, but you're following the Holy Spirit's lead and allowing Him to guide you—so God is the real driver. He gets you where He wants you at just the right time. He only asks you to hop out of the truck and deliver what He wants to say or do for each person. It may be words of love, words of knowledge or words of prophecy. It could be a healing in their body or a miracle in their lives. You don't have to worry or figure out ahead of time what each person needs from God. You simply listen expectantly and by faith hand them their gift.

This lifestyle is truly fun and exhilarating. You'll have the privilege of delivering God's love, and the joy of seeing hearts touched and changed by that love. It's like Christmas all year long.

Here are a few examples of the Holy Spirit directing my GPS truck:

❧*Forgotten Items*❧

I was hustling through my routine in order to get more writing finished before the monthly writer's meeting that afternoon. Sierra was training for her career in massage therapy while completing her senior year of home schooling, so I drove her to the massage school as usual. When we arrived, she realized she had forgotten some necessary items. For just a moment I started to get a little frustrated, but I reminded myself the Holy Spirit is directing my path, and if nothing else, inconveniences are always a good opportunity to grow in patience.

I drove home, grabbed the items and headed back. After giving them to Sierra, I bumped into one of the owners of the school and introduced myself. I told her the school was an answer to prayer and a huge blessing for Sierra since she wanted to have an occupation that helps people. My mentioning *prayer* and using the word *blessing* opened up the doors to a spiritual conversation, and we began talking about the Lord. We talked for almost an hour as she peppered me with God questions, as she called them. I also listened as she shared her heart's desire to help runaway teenagers. When we finished talking, I prayed with her that God would pour out His love and wisdom, and that He would bless her as she blesses runaway teenagers and other people in her life.

After saying good-bye I headed out, hoping to get home quickly to work on my writing, but one of the young ladies in the lobby caught my eye. The Holy Spirit impressed me to talk with her, so I ignored my time crunch and plunged in.

"Hello. My name is Julie," I said.

She told me her name and gave me a warm greeting.

"As I passed you, I sensed the Lord wanted to remind you how special you are to Him," I said. "He sees all you've been through and all you're going through, and every detail of your life is important to Him. I also sense there are some issues with relationships that God wants to help you with, particularly a boyfriend. I feel like God wants to remind you not to settle for less than His best. I've always told each of my daughters to find a man who loves Jesus with all his heart so that he will be able to better love her. None of us have enough love in ourselves. We have to draw from God's love in order to properly love others." She nodded in agreement.

I also felt she had grown up in church, but was floundering spiritually. Wanting to present that information in love, and wanting to make sure I was correct I asked her, "Did you grow up in church?"

"Yes, I went to church with my parents, but my boyfriend and I don't go very often. I can't talk him into going on Sunday mornings as much as I'd like." Her response confirmed what I was feeling about the boyfriend.

We spoke for a few more moments, and I encouraged her that God was going to keep drawing her closer to His heart and giving her wisdom because He loves her so much.

"Thank you," she said with a smile.

"You're very special. Never forget that. God bless you."

We said our good-byes and I left.

So, no, I didn't get as much written as I would have liked that morning, but God used forgotten items to direct my GPS truck on His path, and He wrote His words of love on two amazing ladies' hearts.

❧Sleeping on the Job❧

Three days later I saw God leading again—getting me to the exact place at the exact time I needed to be there. I was staying with my sweet ninety-five-year-old Grandma Taylor (who has since gone to be with Jesus) while my parents, her caregivers, were out of town. I intended to get up early and do some more writing after devotions and a walk, but I was unusually exhausted and fell back to sleep after fixing Grandma her breakfast at 6:00 a.m. I woke up again at 9:00 a.m., checked on Grandma who was watching TV in her room, let out the chickens my parents raised for eggs, and again fell back to sleep. I was shocked when I re-awoke at almost 11:00 a.m. Even if I want to, I almost never fall back to sleep once I'm awake—and this morning I had done it twice. I slept almost eleven hours, which is a minor miracle for me. It was truly strange.

Once I was awake, I read my Bible, visited with Grandma and finally headed on that walk at 1:00 p.m. About twenty minutes into the walk, I saw a middle-aged gentleman come out of his house, get something out of his truck and start to head back inside. As I usually do when I pass people, I asked God to bless and love on this man, and I asked God if He had anything for him. I felt a strong impression that He did, so I called out to the man.

"Hello! This warm winter weather is wonderful, isn't it?" I asked as I began walking into his yard.

"Yes, it is," he responded cheerfully and headed toward me.

"As I was passing your house, I asked God to bless you, and I sensed He wanted to remind you again how much He loves you." The word *heart* came to mind, so I asked, "Is there anything going on with your heart?"

He gave me a surprised look. "I'm as healthy as a horse, but what you may have sensed is that I was just talking with God fifteen minutes ago asking for more patience and grace for the three young children we adopted this year. My wife and I were married later in life and never had children of our own."

How sweet that the Holy Spirit led me to this man at this exact moment to encourage him in his adoption journey. He shared his adoption story and I shared mine. I gave him a few helpful tips the Lord had shown us through the years, and I shared some prophetic words of encouragement and love from the Lord's heart for him and his family.

The man's name was Earl, and he was very appreciative of what I shared and that I had stopped to talk with him. "You are the second person who has come up to me out of the blue to share something from God," he said. "The first person who did that was instrumental in leading me to Christ. I wasn't a Christian, but I had made a deal with God that I would go to church three times if He helped me with the current predicament I was in. He helped me through it, so I made good on my part of the deal. On my third visit at a large church, a man walked up to me and told me he didn't know why he had such an urge to talk to me, but he felt I needed him. He told me God loved me and was ready for me to invite Him into my life. Shortly after that I gave my heart to the Lord, but that man never knew what his boldness did for me. My life was transformed.

"Never underestimate the power of what you are doing by listening to God and talking to people. You won't see all the fruit from your obedience, but lives are being touched and changed—so don't stop." His words were a sweet encouragement. I prayed for him and his family and then gave him a hug good-bye. He invited me to visit any time.

I was chuckling on the rest of my walk. *So that's why I slept like crazy this morning, Holy Spirit. You wanted me to meet Earl at the exact moment he walked out of his house so that I could encourage him and he could encourage me. You're incredible and truly amazing. I guess my sleeping "on the job" was exactly what You wanted in this case.*

❧Sopping with Sweat❧

I was driving out of the First Baptist Church parking lot where I had just done a one-hour intense Boot Camp exercise class. I was make-up-less with unfixed hair and sopping with sweat, but the Holy Spirit impressed on me a man working on some sort of electrical box not far from the church. I almost ignored the prompting since I felt so gross, but I reminded myself that this wasn't about me. I pulled up as close as I could and rolled down my window. I saw that he worked for a local electric company.

"Hello," I called out. The man walked closer to my car as I began to talk with him. "I just wanted you to know how much I sensed God's love over you. He highlighted you to me so that I could remind you of His pleasure in you."

"Thank you," he said with a smile.

I felt he was a believer so I asked, "Are you a believer?"

"Yes!"

I opened my mouth and trusted God was going to fill it, and continued talking. "I could tell. I sense God is going to be moving you into powerful ministry, and I even see you praying for people and they will be healed. God has exciting things in store for you."

"We *are* praying for healing for my grandfather who doesn't have much longer to live," he said. "In fact, my mother was going to talk with him this morning, and she is probably talking with him right now, to make sure he is saved and has a relationship with Jesus."

I immediately jumped into a prayer for his grandfather, not even closing my eyes. It was short and to the point, and I finished with, "Lord, bring him to your heart even now. Touch him with your love."

"Amen!" the man heartily agreed.

We talked a few more minutes. "I'll keep praying for your grandfather when the Lord brings him to mind, but I had better let you get back to work. God bless you."

"Thank you and God bless you, too."

Thank You, Lord, for getting both of us to the same place at the same time. It was only a four-minute conversation, but You encouraged a man who was a stranger to me, but no stranger to You. You allowed me to be a part of his mother's efforts today to reach out to her father before he dies. Bring her father to You, Lord. Break all the lies over his mind and heart that have kept him from Your forgiveness and love. Today is his day of salvation.

❧Wisdom Teeth and Heavenly Wisdom❧

The Holy Spirit not only directs our steps, He directs our conversations. I had driven Dane to the oral surgeon's office early one morning to get his wisdom teeth pulled during his summer break from college classes. When we arrived, there was an Indian gentleman from India waiting in the lobby. We both said, "Hello," and smiled at him, but he was talking on his phone, so Dane and I just chatted with each other. When the man finished on the phone I mentioned to him that Dane was getting his wisdom teeth pulled and asked if he was waiting for someone having their teeth pulled.

"No. I'm not," he said, "but it is interesting that almost everyone in America gets their wisdom teeth pulled whereas in India almost no one does." We talked about that for a few minutes and then I continued the conversation by asking questions.

"How long have you lived in the United States?"

"Eighteen years," he answered.

"Do you go back to visit India often?"

"About every two years my wife, kids and I go back to visit family."

"Is your wife American?"

"No. She's from India. We had an arranged marriage, and then she joined me in America."

"Are arranged marriages still common?"

"About half the marriages are arranged. You have to marry in your social status."

"Is that similar to the caste system?"

"The Hindus follow the caste system," he said. We discussed the Hindu caste system for a few minutes.

"Are you a Hindu?" I asked, excited that the conversation was turning to spiritual matters.

"No. I'm a Muslim."

"We are Christians," I said as I pointed to Dane and myself.

"We have many similarities to Christianity," he said. "We believe Jesus is a prophet and that He will come back one day, but we believe that He was created."

"We believe that Jesus is God," I said with a smile. "God said in Genesis chapter 1, *'Let us make man in our image.'* The Father, Son and Holy Spirit are all One God, but God is so incredible that He manifests in three forms. Jesus said, *'I and the Father are one'*" (John 10:30).

He was listening so I continued. "God is perfect, so sin can't even survive in His presence. Our sin keeps us from God, but because Jesus is God and is perfect, He alone was able to die and take the punishment for our sins. When you ask Jesus to forgive you and live inside you, God's Spirit comes to live in you and you become a new person. That's what happened to us," I again pointed to Dane and myself. "We have been filled with God and His love, so we want to do what pleases Him because we love Him so much. It's not about following rules, but following the desire of your heart when God lives in your heart."

As soon as I finished, the receptionist called his name. He excused himself and went in for his appointment. Shortly after that, Dane was called back to prep for his surgery. About twenty minutes later, the man came back out and walked over to me, so I stood up.

"Thank you," he said with a smile as he shook my hand. "We just have minor differences."

"We believe those differences affect our eternity," I said with warmth and love in my voice and eyes. "Jesus came to pay for our sins, and if we believe in Him and ask Him to forgive us and lead us, then we are forgiven and get to spend eternity in heaven. If we don't, then unfortunately we spend eternity in hell. Please pray and ask God to show you the truth. He loves you, and you are very special to Him! He will talk to you." We shook hands again and he thanked me one more time. "God bless you," I said with a big smile before he turned to leave.

Lord, touch his heart. This meeting and the flow of the conversation was orchestrated by You. Keep softening his heart and mind to Your love and truth. Bring others along who are bold enough to share more of Your love with him and his family. He is truly special to Your heart!

❧My Big Book❧

Four months later I took Sierra to get *her* wisdom teeth pulled by the same doctor, but at another office location. The waiting room was empty, so I read my Bible and discussed in my heart what I was reading with Jesus, thanking Him for all His words of wisdom in the book of Matthew. After twenty minutes, an Indian gentleman (not the same one) entered and filled out paperwork. I asked God to bless him, but didn't say more than "hello" and a comment about the rare ice storm we were still recovering from. When he finished with his paperwork I didn't have any questions pop into my mind for him, so I left it in the Holy Spirit's hands.

I'm available if You want to bless this man through me, Holy Spirit.

Two minutes later, the man spoke to me. "That's a big book you're reading."

I immediately knew this was the Holy Spirit's way of opening the door to share God's love with him, so I plunged in. "This is my Bible and I love reading it…."

We proceeded to have a twenty-minute conversation in which I was able to lovingly share a little of my story and how Jesus died so this man and his family could spend eternity with God. He was a non-practicing Hindu, so I explained the difference between religion with its list of rules, and a relationship with the God who created us and wants to be with us in all we do. I told him how to receive God's forgiveness and begin that relationship. His heart was soft and open, but still full of questions that I'm sure the Holy Spirit will continue to answer. I encouraged him to ask the Lord to show Himself to him and his family, and I gave him my contact information as well as resources to learn more. (I rarely hear from people, but I like to give them the option of contacting me.) Little did this man know that his simple comment about my big book was actually the Holy Spirit's way of opening the door to my GPS truck and releasing a package of love and truth created specifically for him.

The beauty of working for GPS is that you don't have to stress and think of things to say, or contrive a plan to start a conversation. When you feel like your truck is parked and not going anywhere because you have nothing to say, simply tell the Lord you are available and pray for the people around you. God may not have anything for you to deliver, but it could be, as in the case of my Hindu friend, that God not only has something to deliver, but that He will have the person even open the GPS truck door for you.

Chapter Highlights and Application

You can Trust God with Your "Yes!": God is perfect in love and wisdom. You can trust that everything He asks you to do and say is out of love for you. If you have ignored the Holy Spirit's promptings because you trusted Satan's lies rather than God's love, take a few minutes right now to talk with God about this. Make the choice to say, "Yes, Lord, I will trust You and do what You ask no matter how scared I might be. I know You would never lead me to do anything You haven't equipped me for and strengthened me to do."

Write out your commitment to say *yes* (or copy mine from this chapter) and stick it on your fridge or mirror, or place it in your purse or wallet as a reminder. When the Holy Spirit prompts you to share with someone, tell Him, "No more no, Lord. I will say yes!"

Join God's Parcel Service Today: Hop into your GPS truck and enjoy your new job. Just remember—you're delivery only—not manufacturing. The Holy Spirit is working in everyone's lives, so there will be people wherever you go who will be blessed by a gift of love from the Lord. If you are fearful, the simplest way to overcome your fear is to jump out of the truck and get the shock over with. It will be scary for a while, but it will get easier as you see people respond to God's love expressed through you. Anything new is scary, but you have a very BIG God living inside you—so go for it and see what He does.

Part 2

"Yes" in Action

Now let's look at the wonderful gifts in your truck and discover how living a *Yes, Lord* lifestyle doesn't have to be stressful or scary, but can be fun and exciting—even when you face opposition. You'll be encouraged to know that even Peter and Paul missed it at times, but God kept using them powerfully and He'll use you powerfully as well.

Chapter 4

What God Wants to
Say and Do

❧*Healed by His Love*❧

I sat down at the desk in our study and flipped on the computer switch. It was mid-morning, and I should have started my weekly cleaning, but instead I had come up with a number of "important" tasks to help delay my chores. Checking emails sounded like another justifiably worthy task, so I quickly glanced at my inbox. I didn't see anything of interest, so I logged onto Facebook.

I checked one of my groups where we share spiritual insights, praises and prayer needs. My friend, Ronda, whom I had first met back at Vineyard Christian Fellowship many years ago, had posted a prayer need the night before. She openly shared what was on her heart:

Yesterday I twisted my knee that had previously had ACL reconstruction. This morning it was swollen and stiff, and I was hit with fear that I might not be able to walk. I began to cry out to God, literally, with tears streaming down my face because of the pain.

I managed to go to work and limped my way through the day, but when I got home I felt discouraged and sad. I had been deeply troubled lately, and this just added to my distress. The cry of my heart had been for a greater revelation of God's love for me, and now, in the midst of my pain and despair, I was really struggling to feel His love. Even though

He had walked with me through many rough times, proving His love again and again, I needed a fresh, heartfelt awareness—a fresh revelation—of God's love for me. And then in the midst of my pain and hopelessness, He spoke to my heart, "Be still and know that I am God. Be still and know my love...."

The rest of her post faded as I sensed Jesus prompting me to share His words of love with Ronda on Facebook. *Give me your words.* I clicked on the comment section and began typing by faith.

Jesus is saying to you, dear Ronda: You are precious beyond your comprehension. Far more treasured than the finest of diamonds or the rarest of jewels...you are truly one of a kind throughout all generations and all eternity. Your beautiful hair, eyes, face and shape were hand-picked by Me and I love to look at you. Your temperament, strengths and weaknesses were chosen for you because I knew what you would face during your short time on the earth. I wanted you to be well-equipped with your strengths so you would praise Me for them, and to humbly turn to Me in your weaknesses....

I chose your giftings—your love for drawing and creativity, your love for animals, and your nurturing, compassionate heart—because I knew you would make your world, My world, a more beautiful and loving place. I knew that I would be able to express My love to you and through you to a world in desperate need of My love.

Ignore Satan's lies and receive My consuming love for you. My love consumes the lies, doubts and fears, and brings truth, trust and perfect peace. You are My joy, Ronda! I love holding you and doing life with you. Dance with Me and bask in My love for you all day long every day.

I love you with an everlasting love and can't wait until you come home. I still have work for you on earth, so walk in My love and in My confidence. You are on this earth for such a time as this just as Esther was. Keep loving and bringing freedom to the captives and opening the eyes of the blind in your special way. I love you forever and always my beloved Ronda! ~ Jesus

I hit *send*, turned off the computer and headed upstairs to clean my bathroom. *Jesus, may Your words of love not only heal Ronda's heart but her body as well. I haven't seen many healings through my prayers yet, but I could see You healing her as she receives a fresh revelation of Your love and rediscovers how precious she is to You.*

Ronda posted a few hours after my post that God had healed her most of the way through the night. That evening she posted again and said she was 100 percent back to normal and was planning on helping her friend move the next day as planned. She shared the following day that even after a full day of moving her friend's furniture, she was still totally healed. Jesus had been ministering His love and healing to Ronda before I even shared the word He gave me, but the word was a confirmation of His healing love and power in her life. She messaged me:

I just want to thank you for taking the time to send the special word from God to me. I have read it over and over, and it resonates deeper in my heart each time. It's exactly what I needed to hear, and I'm convinced it was the primary instrument in a miraculously speedy recovery to my knee! Thank you!

God's Lavish Love Gifts

Once you begin to listen and say *yes* to the Holy Spirit's promptings, you'll find there is so much He wants to say and do through you. Above all else, He desires to lavish His love. *"How great is the love the Father has lavished on us"* (1 John 3:1). God's lavish love poured in us transforms our lives. God's lavish love poured through us transforms our world.

Just as God lavished His love on Ronda through me with an encouraging prophetic word, a gift from His Spirit, He wants to lavish His love through you with His gifts. Let's look more in-depth at the gifts God has placed in your GPS (God's Parcel Service) truck for you to reach in and grab by faith. You may have been told these gifts aren't available for you, so please read the following verses prayerfully, asking the Holy Spirit to fill you with faith to believe that what He has promised is still true. Jesus said these signs will follow those who believe (see Mark 16:17), and your world desperately needs you to believe!

> *Now there are varieties of gifts, but the same Spirit. And there are varieties of ministries, and the same Lord. There are varieties of effects, but the same God who works all things in all persons. But to each one is given the manifestation of the Spirit for the common good. For to one is given the **word of wisdom** through the Spirit, and to another the **word of knowledge** according to the same Spirit; to another **faith** by the same Spirit, and to another gifts of **healing** by the one Spirit, and to another effecting of **miracles**, and to another **prophecy**, and to another the **distinguishing of spirits**, to another various kinds of **tongues**, and to another the **interpretation of tongues**. But one and the same Spirit works all these things, distributing to each one individually just as He wills.*
>
> 1 Corinthians 12:4-11 (NASB, emphasis mine)

I love how God *"works all things in all persons"* (verse 6). God wants to give each of the gifts to all His children at various times as needed. On one delivery you might have a word of knowledge about something from a person's past. On the next delivery you might have a prophecy about something in another person's future. The next day you may pray for someone and they are healed. (I'm anxious to see more of that in my life!) The exciting part is that no one has to be left out. *"To each one is given the manifestation of the Spirit"* (verse 7). Each one of us is meant to receive and share these gifts. To emphasize this point, it is repeated again in verse 11: *"But one and the same Spirit works all these things, distributing to each one individually just as He wills."* He distributes these gifts to each of us. Your GPS truck is filled with them so that you can lavish God's love on the world. It's simply a matter of stepping out by faith and believing God will speak and work through you. Just as salvation is received by faith, these gifts are received—and accessed—by faith.

Peeking in the Truck

Once you say *yes* to God's promptings, you'll be operating in the gifts of the Spirit regularly. The gifts aren't scary or weird, but incredibly sweet and powerful. Let's take a peek in the truck and look more closely at the gifts before you step out by faith to deliver them.

WORDS OF WISDOM

God will gift you with words of wisdom, revelation and insight. Sometimes God's Spirit will remind you of Bible verses, past teachings or words He's already spoken to your heart. But He will also gift you with words of wisdom that come directly from His heart and apply specifically to your current situation or to the need of the person you are talking with. The Holy Spirit will often download to your thoughts what the person needs to hear to guide or encourage them through their situation. You have probably shared words of wisdom from God's heart many times in the past, but may not have been aware that it was God speaking through you.

Ron and I faced a difficult parenting situation recently where we needed supernatural words of wisdom to guide our steps because our next course of action would have serious challenges whichever route we chose. We fell asleep asking the Holy Spirit to guide us, and the following morning we woke up knowing what we were supposed to do. We both had clear direction from the Lord with the steps we needed to take. Even though God was asking us to go the harder route, we have already seen in hindsight that the wisdom He poured into our thoughts was definitely the best decision for everyone involved.

WORDS OF KNOWLEDGE

Words of knowledge are simply facts God knows about someone that He shares with you to share with them to prove He knows and loves them. This could be things from their past or present such as details about their childhood or a current challenge they are battling. When you ask God to give you a word of knowledge for someone, you have to step out by faith and speak what comes to mind, or just begin speaking and allow God to put the words in your mouth. You won't always be correct (I talk about that in the next chapter), but God loves your faith in His ability to speak, and He is honored that you are willing to take risks to love people for Him. As your faith increases and you take more risks, your ability to hear will increase.

Jesus had two words of knowledge for Nathanael in John 1:47-48. He had a word of knowledge about Nathanael's character, *"Here is a true Israelite, in whom there is nothing false,"* and he had a word of knowledge about where Nathaniel had just been. *"'How do you know me?' Nathaniel asked. Jesus answered, 'I saw you while you were still under the fig tree before Philip called you.'"* These two words were simple, but they rocked Nathanael's world. Words don't have to be detailed to be profound.

❧ On God's Heart ❧

I try to give words of knowledge, no matter how simple they seem, whenever I can. One day I was buying groceries and stopped to chat with an unmarried couple who had a cute two-year-old boy. I asked the Holy Spirit if He had anything for them. I sensed the young man had been an on-fire believer when he was a teenager, but he had drifted from the Lord. I try not to present any of my words in a negative light because God is about loving people, so I told him that I felt he had been very on-fire for the Lord as a teenager and that God was relighting that fire in Him and was going to use him powerfully. The man shook his head when I said this, agreeing with my words. I continued to share more thoughts from the Holy Spirit as they popped into my head. They were simple words of knowledge, but I could tell the young man was impacted.

Just a few minutes after we spoke, I met another young couple with a baby. As I oohed and aahed over their baby, I breathed a quick prayer asking the Holy Spirit to show me something for them. I looked up from the baby and saw God's love shining in the man's eyes. I saw God's tenderness, and it surprised me how clear it was that this man was a believer and filled with the Holy Spirit. God was opening *my* eyes and I was excited. I looked at his wife and didn't see the same thing in her eyes.

I immediately asked him, "Are you a Christian?"

"Yes!"

"I can see the Lord shining through your eyes," I said. We continued to talk, and I shared some more words from the Lord that encouraged him. During the conversation, he sweetly mentioned his wife was struggling with the whole Christianity thing.

I was amazed I had already seen the difference through their eyes. This had never happened before, although it's happened many times since.

Thoughts came to me for his wife, so I shared them. God spoke to her past pain and her current doubt, and He encouraged her that she would soon know His love deep in her heart. The conversation lasted less than five minutes and then I prayed a short prayer with them. I sensed God had touched them deeply in those few minutes as He made it clear He knew them and loved them. The beauty of giving words of knowledge is that people see firsthand that they are on God's heart and are truly special to Him.

FAITH

The gift of faith encompasses all the other gifts because a gift of faith can cause salvation, healing, miracles, tongues or prophetic words. Some believe a gift of faith is just for a moment or a particular instance, but I believe God wants us to carry around and use the gift of faith in everything we do. Just as you can operate in the prophetic everywhere you go, you can operate in faith everywhere you go. You and I can live in the childlike faith many of us sang about at the top of our lungs in Sunday School: "Our God is so BIG, so STRONG and so MIGHTY, there's nothing our God cannot do!"

HEALING

God made our bodies to miraculously heal themselves naturally, but the gift of healing is a "super" natural recovery from an illness, injury or disease. The healing could come in multiple stages as your faith grows, or it could come immediately.

I've seen a few immediate healings at this point. Several years ago I prayed for a homeless woman whose foot was hurting, and as soon as I prayed she said, "How'd you do that? The pain's gone!"

Another time I was with Dane, and we both prayed for an employee at McDonalds who had back pain and one leg shorter than the other. We watched her leg realign and stretch out as we prayed, and she said her back pain lessened. Another time I was at a conference and received prayer for my ankle that had been injured years earlier and had become inflexible and sporadically painful. When they prayed, my ankle immediately loosened, and it rarely hurts. Another time I was in a meeting and felt the Lord prompt me that He was healing head issues, thyroids, hormones and female issues, so I shared that word. My messed up thyroid had been keeping me from remembering song lyrics from the past or present for several years, and I ached that I couldn't sing throughout the day like I had my whole life. On the way home from the meeting I began singing and was able to remember song after song, and I was tickled pink. This was a huge gift to me!

There are still numerous health issues where we need healing breakthrough for myself and family members, but I see it coming very soon. I know God doesn't want us sick. Just look at how much time Jesus spent healing while He was on the earth—and Jesus' mission was to reveal the Father's heart to the world.

Heidi Baker,[6] Bill Johnson and Sandra Kennedy[7] are among many who are seeing healings and are teaching others how to grow in their faith and see healings for themselves. Not everyone they pray for is healed, but many people have had cancer cells vanish, blind eyes open, deaf ears hear, dead people raised to life and numerous other serious diseases or injuries completely restored.

When our son, Dane, was in Africa, he and Heidi Baker prayed for a partially blind woman who was instantly healed. Dane also witnessed several deaf, crippled and lame people healed. Another group with his team prayed for a four-year-old little girl who was healed and able to walk for the first time in her life. The Africans don't have as many doctors to turn to, so it's easier for them to put their faith in God rather than doctors or medicine as we do in the Western world.

Bill Johnson teaches that we must know who God is—the Healer—and know who we are—God's mighty children. We have the same incomparably great power in us that raised Christ from the dead (see Ephesians 1:18-20). That's a lot of power!

Sandra Kennedy teaches that our minds are like filters that get clogged up with lies from Satan telling us God won't heal or doesn't want to heal. We must rebuke and silence Satan's lies and allow God's truth to clean out our filters for faith and healing to flow.

The disciples' filters were clogged with lies from Satan when they prayed for a demon-possessed boy and he wasn't healed. When they asked Jesus why they couldn't drive out the demon, *"He replied, 'Because you have so little faith. I tell you the truth, if you have faith as small as a mustard seed, you can say to this mountain, 'Move from here to there' and it will move. Nothing will be impossible for you"* (Matthew 17:20-21). When the disciples' prayers didn't heal the boy, they could have surmised that it wasn't God's will to heal him, but Jesus blew that theory out of the water when He turned and healed the boy himself. It's not God's will that we be sick. It's just that we, like the disciples, need to do what it takes to stop believing the lies of Satan. We need to soak God's words of truth because *"faith comes by hearing, and hearing by the word of God"* (Romans 10:17 NKJV).

No matter where your faith level currently is, I encourage you to pray for people in need of healing wherever you go. Faith is increased by taking risks. We saw the disciples' faith grow as they continued to pray for people. Even if the person you pray for isn't healed, they will be blessed that you cared enough to stop and pray for them. Just don't give up. Keep seeking the Lord for healing and for greater faith. *"Without faith it is impossible to please God, because anyone who comes to Him must believe that He exists and that He rewards those who earnestly seek him"* (Hebrews 11:6). Don't stress, but stay earnest because your growing faith pleases God and it will be rewarded as you immerse yourself in His truth.

MIRACLES

Miracles are supernatural acts of God like the ones we saw Jesus perform such as multiplying food, walking on water, calming the storm and turning water into wine. Since Jesus said we would do greater things than He did, we need to expect miracles in our lives and pray for miracles in others' lives on a daily basis. We can expect miracles of provision, protection and blessing because we are God's beloved children.

Sometimes these miracles will be obvious, and other times God will work supernaturally behind the scenes. I have not yet seen food multiply physically before my eyes as Heidi Baker has seen happen for her orphans, but I have seen God provide supernaturally. Even while writing this book, we saw God's miraculous provision. Ron had serious health issues at the beginning of 2013 that put him out of work for several months, and then working reduced hours for the rest of the year. My going to work wasn't the best of options right then, and when we asked the Lord if I should get a job other than the occasional event staffing jobs, He told both Ron and I *no.* The Holy Spirit made it clear that He would provide, and our hearts were at peace as we trusted Him.

True to His word, God did provide in miraculous ways. Several people randomly gave us money or food; my 98-year-old Grandma Neidig went to be with Jesus and left all the grandkids a little money; stocks from several sources that hadn't been worth anything in years suddenly became valuable, and we cashed them in; and the IRS informed us our electronically-filed tax return from the previous year had not been received by them as we thought, so they sent us our tax return that we somehow hadn't noticed we didn't get the year before. This is not to mention all the small provisions through deals and discounts we found at thrift stores and grocery stores. Dollars stretched in amazing ways that we never would have thought of on our own. We may not have had money appear in our pockets, but God miraculously provided in every way.

God is not done working miracles because the world isn't done needing miracles. Expect miracles wherever you go and watch what God does. Remember, He won't do them if you don't ask for and expect them. *"You do not have because you do not ask God"* (James 4:2). So ask and keep asking. *"For everyone who asks receives…. If you…know how to give good gifts to your children, how much more will your Father in heaven give good gifts to those who ask Him!"* (Matthew 7:8-11).

DISTINGUISHING OF SPIRITS

Distinguishing of spirits is the ability to recognize the difference between our spirit, demonic spirits and God's Spirit, and to discern what type of demonic spirit is at work in a situation. Ephesians 6:12

says: *"For our struggle is not against flesh and blood, but against the rulers, against the authorities, against the powers of this dark world and against the spiritual forces of evil in the heavenly realms."* We are in a war, so as you go about your day, ask God to reveal if there are specific strongholds in people's lives as you pray for them. Demons will hassle and attack both Christians and non-Christians with their lies. Walking in willful sin and believing demonic lies opens doors for demonic attacks in our lives. The lies could be anything opposite God's truth such as: God doesn't love me, God can't be trusted, I'm not special, no one cares about me, my actions don't matter, sin is okay…and on and on.

You have the same power Jesus had, so tell the demons to be silent and be gone. This doesn't need to be crazy or weird. Just calmly claim your territory and command the enemy and his harassing lies to go in Jesus' name. Know your authority and walk in it.

TONGUES

I discussed the gift of tongues in Chapter 1. It's not weird, but simply a sweet way for our spirits to pray as the Holy Spirit prays through us. It gets our thoughts out of the way so that God can pray His thoughts. When you are around other people who don't understand this gift and you feel prompted to pray in your prayer language, it's usually a good idea to pray under your breath or in your head since they won't understand what is happening, and you may distract them from what the Holy Spirit is doing in their hearts.

If you're praying with a group who does understand this precious gift, then praying quietly in your prayer language while others take turns praying in English is truly beneficial because it helps you tune in to what the Holy Spirit is saying and doing.

There was a news story done on ABC News titled *Speaking in Tongues: Alternative Voices in Faith* by Vicki Mabrey and Roxanna Sherwood. It was posted on the Internet on March 20, 2007. This is one of many stories where scientists did brain scans when a person was talking or listening to gospel music and then while they prayed in tongues. Brain activity in the frontal lobes increased when they talked or listened to music, but decreased and even went quiet when they prayed in tongues. The scientists tested the brains of

Buddhist Monks meditating and Franciscan Nuns praying, thinking it might be a similar phenomenon, but the monks' and nuns' frontal lobes increased in activity while they meditated and prayed, just as they do when any conscious thought is taking place.

It makes sense that our brain's control center decreases in activity or goes quiet while we pray in tongues. We aren't formulating the words—God is. And when God is praying, you know those prayers are incredibly powerful and effective.

INTERPRETATION OF TONGUES

Interpretation of tongues is God gifting you with an understanding of what someone prayed in their prayer language. It's not necessarily a word-for-word translation, although it could be. It may be more a sense of what the Spirit is expressing so you are able to share that with the group in English. This would be hard to verify in most cases unless the tongue was in a language someone understood. According to the Bible, though, tongues can be either a heavenly language or an earthly language, so not every language can be verified. *"If I speak in the tongues of men and of angels"* (1 Corinthians 13:1). Ask the Holy Spirit to show you if the interpretation was correct or not. He will confirm it in other ways if it was.

PROPHECY

Most often we think of prophecy in relation to something coming up in the future, and that's true part of the time, but all words that come from the Lord fall under the term *prophecy*. According to Dictionary.com, prophecy is "a divinely inspired prediction, instruction or exhortation." The term is not limited to foretelling of the future, but includes instruction and encouragement. In the Old Testament, a prophet would give a prophecy that told the people what they had done (a word of knowledge), what they should be doing (a word of wisdom) and the consequences they would face if they didn't repent and change (a foretelling of the future). In the New Testament, we see prophecy used as an all-inclusive term as well. First Corinthians 14:24-25 talks about a nonbeliever coming into a meeting as people are prophesying and the *"secrets of his heart will be laid bare. So he will fall down and worship God, exclaiming, 'God is really among you!'"* Prophecy in this instance is referring to giving a word of knowledge as God reveals things from a person's life. They usually aren't bad things, because that wouldn't be edifying, but they are facts or perhaps dreams they have in their heart.

Whether the prophecy is a word of wisdom, a word of knowledge or a foretelling, the goal of prophecy is *"so that everyone may be instructed and encouraged"* (1 Corinthians 14:31). Since the purpose of prophecy is for instruction and encouragement, if you feel like you have a word on your GPS route and it isn't going to provide help or inspiration, then it may not be from the Lord.

If your word is corrective, be sure to present it positively. For example, if you feel the Lord is calling someone out of a bad relationship, don't say, "You're in a bad relationship and you need to get out." Instead you might say something like, "You've had some tough challenges with relationships, but the Holy Spirit is empowering you to choose wisely and to step into relationships that will build you up and encourage you in your walk with the Lord."

If you feel someone is struggling with pornography, don't blurt it out rudely and shame him or her. Take the person aside privately and present what you are feeling with a gentle, kind posturing, not being too specific in case you're wrong or so as not to embarrass the person. Say something like, "I sense there has been an area in your life where the enemy has been lying to you and getting victory in your life. The Lord is calling you to freedom and victory in the mighty name of Jesus. The Lord is drawing you into such a radical love relationship with Him that all temptations of the enemy will lose even a shred of enticement in the presence of that love. Run into His love and find your strength. You are the righteousness of God in Christ Jesus. You are an overcomer!" Focus on the power of God and the person's upcoming victory rather than their current defeat. Give them God's vision for their victorious future.

Do everything in your power not to embarrass people. Giving a critical word, whether accurate or inaccurate, can do more harm than good. When our daughter, Richelle, was a teenager, there was a speaker visiting her youth group who was usually correct when he gave prophetic words. The teenagers were all waiting for their turn to receive a word from him, and it was taking quite a while. Richelle was tired and kept shifting on her feet even when it was her turn for a word. The man saw her body language and made a judgment rather than hearing a word from the Lord. He told her that she was rebellious, when nothing could be further from the truth. This inaccurate word, spoken in front of the other youth, embarrassed and hurt Richelle.

I called him a couple days later to kindly but firmly tell him he was wrong, and that he handled it improperly by publicly speaking a negative word. He apologized, and I made sure to learn from his mistake.

I also try to be very careful with words that give specific life-changing direction because I know I'm human and am sometimes wrong. I rarely give words that include dates, mates or babies. If I do, I try to be vague and remind the person that I make mistakes. I ask them to pray about the word and allow the Holy Spirit to confirm it in their hearts and in other ways. If it's the Lord, then He will use a variety of methods to make sure the message is clearly validated. This validation happens with all believers who are listening and paying attention.

Called to Speak and Write

One instance of clear validation happened to me in 1999 while I was at a women's retreat. I was listening to the guest speaker during one of the sessions when out of the blue the strong thought came to me, *"You will be doing what she is doing one day."* The thought was so spontaneous and strong that I was pretty confident it was the Lord's voice.

You mean I'll be speaking, Lord? I had a passion for missions and sharing Jesus with people, but I had never once thought about being a conference speaker or any sort of speaker for that matter. As I sat there, my inadequacies flooded my thoughts and I listed them:

Lord, You know my memory seems to be getting worse.
My marriage, while much better, is still far from perfect.
I had to work hard for my good grades in school—
surely others could better share Your truths....

But You love me and know what's best for me,
So please confirm this word in several ways this weekend if it's You.

As a specific confirmation, let me talk with the retreat speaker privately before the retreat is over.

I knew it would take God stepping in supernaturally for me to talk with the speaker since there were 160 women at the retreat, and the speaker was usually praying or studying in her room. But I knew it would be easy for God if He was truly calling me to speak.

The next morning I sat by the lake to read my Bible. I had been reading in Ezekiel, but I felt led to read in Acts. I randomly opened to Acts chapter 4 and glanced down. I read verse 13 and a thrill that gave me goose bumps shot through my body. *"When they saw the courage of Peter and John and realized that they were unschooled, ordinary men, they were astonished and they took note that these men had been with Jesus."* Peter and John didn't work hard for their good grades—they hadn't even gone to school. They were ordinary men who probably didn't have great memories or perfect marriages, yet God used them powerfully because they had been with Jesus. Their power came from relationship and intimacy with the Lord.

I felt the Father whisper to my heart, *"Just be with Me and I'll take care of the rest."*

Thank You, sweet Father. I'll focus on loving You and let You work out the details.

God used other conversations and events during the retreat to further confirm His word, but as the weekend was coming to a close, I still hadn't been able to talk with the speaker. She finished speaking during the Sunday morning session and then sat down in the row in front of me. Normally we would have a breakout session with our small groups to discuss the topic, but this time they said there would be a ten-minute break before the speaker shared for the final time. I knew this was my answer to prayer, so I quickly got up and knelt down in front of her before she had time to stand up. I told her what I felt God had spoken to my heart and the concerns I had. She said she had a bad memory, too, and that she and her husband still didn't have a perfect marriage, but that God doesn't expect perfection in order to use us to help others on their journey. She suggested I keep a journal and gave several other tips. I only kept her for five minutes, but I knew God had ordained that five-minute conversation to give me the encouragement I needed.

After the retreat was over, I didn't rush out and try to make this prophetic word come to pass. I trusted God to work out the details. I was busy doing my most important life's work—being a wife and mother, and raising the next generation to know God intimately. This word from the Lord, though, did help me prioritize my extra time. I took advantage of books and conferences for speakers when they became available, and I kept journals (although somewhat sporadically) of the lessons the Holy Spirit taught me that might one day help others.

Several years later, a Christian women's magazine arrived in our mailbox that a friend had signed me up to receive as a gift. In it was an advertisement for the *Christian Writer's Guild* two-year writer's training program. I was excited and immediately knew in my spirit this was my next step. In that moment, God spoke to my heart that I would be writing books one day. Although I have always enjoyed writing, tackling a book sounded overwhelming, but I trusted God would direct my path and give me grace step by step if it was His will.

And here I am, almost sixteen years later, with this first book completed and with the incredible privilege of sharing the truth of God's love at conferences and retreats in the U.S. and overseas. I've had fun watching the Holy Spirit direct the whole process, gradually fulfilling the prophetic words He gave me. I didn't have to strive, stress or push to make things happen. I simply had to trust God and do my best to follow His lead moment by moment.

Prophecy Isn't a Scary Word

Please don't allow the word *prophecy* to make you nervous. Prophecy is simply listening for God's words to your thoughts and then sharing those words with others. Most Christians realize God speaks to their thoughts to direct and encourage them personally, but they don't realize God wants to speak to their thoughts to bless and encourage others. Once we recognize God is speaking to us for others, our job is to listen expectantly and take leaps of faith to share what we hear.

As a side note, don't be nervous around people who listen for God's voice. I used to be uncomfortable around prophetic people because I thought they knew if I had argued with my husband that day or snapped at my kids.

When I'm listening for God's voice, I rarely hear about the negative things in someone's life. If I do, I share those things lovingly and in light of what God wants to do to bring victory. God isn't about airing people's dirty laundry—He's about building us up in love. You can trust Him not to share more than is absolutely necessary to best love you and encourage you in your growth.

⁓❦⁓

For a more in-depth look at prophecy and the gifts of the Spirit, I would encourage you to read these insightful and enjoyable books by Douglas Banister, Jack Deere and Mike Bickle:

The Word and Power Church by Dr. Douglas Banister[8]

This is a great book, especially if you aren't sure the Holy Spirit is still blessing the church with His gifts. Dr. Banister, a pastor and seminary graduate, uses historical facts and Scripture to lovingly encourage believers to break down the walls between Evangelicals and Charismatics and combine the strengths of both traditions—the deep study of the Word and a hunger for more of God's presence and power to change lives.

Surprised by the Power of the Spirit by Jack Deere[9]

Jack received His doctorate of theology, but he eventually realized his views on the Holy Spirit were based more on prejudice and lack of personal experience than on the Bible. Once he became a seeker instead of a skeptic, the Holy Spirit revealed Himself in new and surprising ways.

Growing in the Prophetic by Mike Bickle[10]

Mike's journey from hating Charismatics to becoming one is humorous and thought provoking. This book is packed with practical tips for hearing God, ideas for working with and training people in the church and warnings of potential abuses when people begin to grow in the gifts.

Chapter Highlights and Application

Lavish God's Love Through His Gifts: If you are wondering how in the world you can pass out all those amazing gifts listed in 1 Corinthians 12—giving words of wisdom, knowledge and prophecy; believing for healing and miracles; distinguishing between demonic and angelic spirits; praying in a different language and interpreting others' languages—then turn your focus off the gifts and on to the Gift Giver. Don't be overwhelmed and paralyze yourself. Honestly tell the Lord where your faith level is and ask Him to increase your faith in His gifts and in His power to use you. Receive His lavish love for you and then pass it along through the gifts He offers. Share His gifts with friends you converse with on the Internet, people shopping near you at the mall, the gal sitting beside you in geometry and the ornery little neighbor boy next door. Start where you're at and keep growing in your use of the gifts.

Become a Student of the Holy Spirit: It's crucial to learn all you can about the Holy Spirit. He isn't some unattached, spooky entity floating around that you rarely think about or interact with. The Holy Spirit is God's Spirit living in you. Second Peter 1:3 says, *"His divine power has given us everything we need for life and godliness through our knowledge of Him...."* How do you get everything you need for life and godliness? Through your knowledge of God. When you get to know the Holy Spirit you'll find out all the *everythings* He intends you to have. Don't settle for a powerless Christian life. Become a student of the Holy Spirit and discover the power and gifts He longs to give you. It will be a thrilling, lifelong discovery uncovering the treasures of His heart and will.

Chapter 5

Step Out in Confidence

❧ Lost Job ❧

It was a lovely Texas day in May, and Sierra and I were running errands. Our last stop was at the Vehicle Registration Office to renew my van's registration. We got in line and were prepared for a long wait, but the lady behind the Title Transfer sign didn't have any customers, so she called us over and greeted us. I returned the greeting and handed her my registration papers.

"May I see your license, please?" she asked.

"Certainly!" I pulled my license out of my wallet and handed it to her. "This picture is from my B.R.H. days—my Before Red Hair days," I chuckled and kept talking. "That must be why they don't ask for hair color on our license any longer because those of us who keep changing the color."

She laughed. "Yes. My husband is bald so he's wondering how he would answer that question of hair color. Would he list *none* or *bald*?" We both laughed.

As she and I interacted, I shot up a quick prayer. *Holy Spirit, do you have anything for this sweet lady?* A few moments later, the thought came to me that something big was happening with her and her husband this summer. I didn't know what was happening. Perhaps I should have listened longer, but she had just finished with the paperwork and handed me my receipt so I was out of time.

Satan whispered into my ear that I couldn't hear God, but I ignored him and leaned over her desk a little. Lowering my voice, I asked, "Are you going on vacation this summer?"

"No," she answered.

"The reason I asked is that I often pray for people when I'm interacting with them, and as I was praying for you I sensed that something big was happening this summer that I should pray about."

"Oh!" she said with surprise as her eyes widened. "My husband is losing his job. Today is his last day and we've been praying God's will would be done in our finances and in directing his path. That's what the big thing is."

There were three customers behind me now, so I couldn't talk long. "So you guys are believers?"

"Yes!"

"I'll be praying God will give your husband the perfect job."

"Thank you!" She told me his name and gave me a few quick details before we said good-bye. Her face glowed with sweet appreciation for this little gift from the Lord.

I prayed out loud as Sierra and I walked to the car. "Lord, pour out your blessings, favor and supernatural leading for her and her husband. Bring the perfect job in your perfect timing."

I was glad I had stepped out of my GPS truck and taken the risk. If I had believed Satan's lies and not said anything, this woman and her husband would have missed out on the encouragement the Holy Spirit wanted to give them through this simple word of knowledge.

You Can Hear God

The greatest deterrent to signing up for God's Parcel Service is believing you can't hear God or be led by God. Satan will constantly throw those lies at you. If you believe the lies, you are inadvertently agreeing with Satan that God isn't powerful enough to communicate with you or through you. It must be extremely painful for God when you and I minimize His power to such a degree that we believe He can't easily talk with His own children.

John 8:47 says, *"He who belongs to God hears what God says. The reason you do not hear is that you do not belong to God."* If you have given your heart and life to God, then you belong to God. If you belong to God, then you can hear what God says!

It's important to stop focusing on your inability and begin focusing on God's ability. When you acknowledge how amazing and powerful God is, you can step out of the delivery truck with confidence. You may not have a clue what you're going to say to someone, but you can start speaking and allow the Holy Spirit to guide you.

> *If anyone speaks, he should do it as one speaking the very words of God.*
>
> —1 Peter 4:11

Wow! You may want to read this verse a number of times before moving on. You are told to speak as if you are speaking the very words of God. This is one of the most important concepts in this book. This is where you choose to believe God and open your mouth by faith and begin speaking, or you choose not to believe God and keep silent.

SATAN WANTS YOU TO STAY IN THE TRUCK

Satan will do everything in his power to convince you 1 Peter 4:11 is a lie. He will constantly whisper his deceptions in your ear: "God can't speak through your lips." "Who do you think you are anyway?" "It's arrogant to believe God can speak through you in the same way He spoke through Jesus, Peter or Paul."

On the contrary, believing that God is eager and able to flow His words through you isn't arrogance—it's true humility. It's knowing God is so completely awesome and mighty that your inadequacies are nothing in comparison with His adequacies. It's walking in pure, child-like faith because you know who your Daddy is and what He is capable of accomplishing through you.

I often hear lies from the enemy telling me I can't hear God as well as other people, and that I'm not up to the task as a delivery person. While I'm comfortable giving words of love, wisdom and encouragement, and praying for people, I'm not always as confident giving detailed and specific words of knowledge. After I missed it on several attempts, Satan was urging me to give it up. He was enticing me to stay in the truck where it's safe, and not take risks to share God's gifts with the world. Even though the door was opened to share God's love with people in spite of wrong or partially correct words, Satan still came at me full force to discourage me. Knowing Satan is nothing but a liar, I took those thoughts captive unto the obedience of Christ as I'm told to do in 2 Corinthians 10:5.

I spoke the truth instead:

Satan is a liar and the father of lies. Jesus said in John 14:12 that "anyone who has faith in me will do what I have been doing. He will do even greater things than these because I am going to the Father."

I choose to have faith in Jesus and speak His words of love to my world. I choose to be a believer who believes the whole Bible. I won't cut out the uncomfortable parts or the parts that require leaping out by faith rather than sight. I will speak what comes to my lips for people, and when I miss it, I'll keep speaking what I hear until I become a fine-tuned listener of the Holy Spirit.

I'll risk being wrong and looking stupid in order to have the chance of being right. I'll believe for detailed words of knowledge and prophecy, to see the sick healed, the dead raised and captives set free from demonic strongholds. Get behind me, Satan! I choose to ignore your lies, doubts and fears, and believe Jesus' promises.

After my face-off with Satan and his lies, I told the Lord I was going all the way and stepping out in confidence no matter how many times I missed it. I would keep reaching into the truck to get the correct gifts rather than clamming up and moving on.

My problem is that I often stop when I get an incorrect word rather than continuing to risk and share other things that come to my thoughts. I still share God's words of love, but I stop trying to hear specific details about their lives. When I do this, I'm robbing them of treasures from the Father. When I do get a word wrong, or even a word that's correct, I need to reach back into the truck and keep looking for other gifts from the Holy Spirit. My tendency is to rush things, but I am learning to slow down and listen longer.

❧Handcuffed❧

With fresh determination to walk in confidence and listen for more details in people's lives, I headed out for my weekly grocery shopping. I picked up my Aunt Patricia and we headed to the store. We passed by a police car and two police officers in the parking lot. One officer was standing in front of the car and the other was sitting in the driver's seat. A young gentleman was in handcuffs leaning against another car, and a young man and woman were standing nearby. The young woman was trying to reach someone on her cell phone and they all appeared to be waiting. I parked near them, and as I got out of the van I felt the nudge, *"Go talk with them."*

I didn't have any idea what I was going to say, but I obeyed and walked toward them. When I got close, the young officer standing outside the car asked, "Can we help you?"

"I don't mean to interrupt," I said, and then I turned to face the three young people, "but when I drove past you I felt like God wanted me to remind you how important you are to Him. He knows everything you've been through, and He is going to give you wisdom and guidance as you look to Him. He has good things for your future as you draw near to His heart and seek Him in all you do." I shared a few more encouraging words and then finished by pointing my finger to the sky and smiling, "He wants you to look up and trust Him."

They had been staring at me, looking rather shocked as I spoke. But when I finished, the young man in handcuffs and the young lady both said, "Thank you," and smiled. The officer just stood there still somewhat dumbfounded.

"God bless you," I said as I started to walk away. "Always remember you are loved."

I hadn't given any detailed words of knowledge, but having never interrupted in the middle of an arrest, I was happy with my risk level. I continued to pray for them as I headed into the store.

❧Mascara❧

My first stop was in the makeup section to get some mascara. When I turned into the correct aisle, there were two ladies discussing what to buy. I prayed God's blessings over them and had the thought that someone was in the hospital in their family.

"How are you ladies today?" I asked with my normal cheeriness.

"We're good," they responded.

"Do you have someone in your family who's in the hospital?"

"No. Not that we know of. Everyone is nice and healthy," the older lady replied.

"That's good. I was just praying God would bless you as I walked past, and that thought came to mind. I'm trying to hear from the Lord as I pray for people, but I don't always get it right."

Her eyes lit up with excitement. "That's so great you pray for people you pass. We are very blessed by the Lord with good health."

"Ah, you are believers, too?"

"Yes!" they both said with enthusiasm. "God has been good to us in so many ways."

We talked for a few minutes about the goodness of God and not wanting to do life without Him. As we began to move on, the older lady looked into my eyes and said, "Thank you for being bold enough to talk with strangers about God."

After saying good-bye, I realized I forgot to listen for more specific words for them after missing it on the initial impression. But I sensed God was stirring their hearts to begin listening and passing out packages themselves, so I wasn't too disappointed with myself.

❧The Love of a Mother❧

Next I headed to the personal care section. I bumped into a friend from a church we had attended six or seven years before. We hadn't seen each other in a long time, so we talked for over ten minutes near the deodorant. While we talked, a young mentally challenged man, probably in his late twenties, was sniffing almost every deodorant on the shelf, trying to decide which one to buy. A nice-looking, white-haired lady who appeared to be his mother waited patiently at the end of the aisle the whole time.

When I finished my conversation with my friend, I turned to the young man and patted him on the back as I smiled at him. "There are a lot of great scents to choose from, aren't there?"

"Yes, there are," he smiled back.

"Well, God bless you."

"Thank you."

I felt a prompting from the Holy Spirit that He wanted to honor the young man's mother. I pushed my cart near her at the end of the row. "Hi. I just had a strong sense the Lord wanted to bless and honor you for all the years you have given to serve and love him," I said as I nodded toward her son.

Tears pooled in her eyes. "I'm sorry. I'm getting teary," she said quietly.

"Don't be sorry. I cry all the time. The Lord loves your tender heart and how patiently you have ministered to your son. You have given up many of your own desires in life to care for him, and God honors you for that. It hasn't been easy on you or your family, but you have done a phenomenal job and delighted God's heart." Her eyes teared up again. "My name is Julie, by the way."

She told me her name and her son's name, who had finally decided on a deodorant with a bright floral design on it, and was now headed to the next aisle to check out different shampoos. "Thank you for your encouraging words. It has been a tremendous challenge." We continued to talk about her son and how he is now living in a group home and doing well. I could tell she was a Christian from her comments, and asked if they were able to be around other Christians for support.

"He has no self-control when it comes to eating, so when we take him to church he gets up in the middle of the service and gets into the church's fridge. It makes it tough to attend." I invited her to try our church since I hadn't noticed an accessible fridge, and the louder, lively music would probably keep him distracted from food.

We wrapped up our conversation and I said good-bye to both of them after giving her my contact information and a big hug. I waved to her son. "Good-bye. Jesus loves you very much. God bless you!"

"Thank you," he gave me a big grin and then quickly turned back to the current shampoo he was investigating.

"God bless you," I said to his mother.

"Thank you again. Your words encouraged me. God bless you, too," she said with a sweet smile on her face.

⊱*Delayed Obedience*⊰

In the produce section, I saw one of the employees I had come to know pretty well since I spend a lot of time picking out produce every week. I greeted him and asked how he was doing. He mentioned how tired he was from working several jobs, and I told him I'd be praying he found time to get plenty of sleep. "God bless you," I said as I walked over to the oranges and put a bag in my cart. I didn't feel any promptings to say more, but as I picked out fruits and vegetables I prayed for him.

I prayed blessings on most of the people I passed in the aisles, asking God to draw each of them to His loving heart, but I didn't get any impressions to say more than the normal "hello" until I got to the canned tomatoes. While looking for stewed tomatoes, I passed a gray-haired man who looked to be in his sixties. I had the thought that God had given him dreams when he was a young man and that God was still going to fulfill those dreams. The aisle got crowded and I didn't jump on the impression immediately. I walked out of the crowd thinking the man would come my way, but instead he turned and headed the opposite direction. When he got to the end of the aisle, he turned to go to the front of the store whereas I was headed toward the back.

I'm sorry, Lord. Delayed obedience is disobedience. Please forgive me for not jumping on Your prompting immediately. Please have grace for this man and allow me to bump into him again if You want me to deliver a message from Your heart. I knew God would have to do it because I rarely see people twice once we head the opposite direction at the grocery store.

I must admit, I was surprised ten minutes later when I turned into the snack aisle near the back of the store and the man was standing there picking out chips. As soon as I saw him, I jumped right in. "When I saw you earlier I felt like God was telling me He gave you dreams when you were a young man and you haven't seen those dreams come true yet. God has not forgotten those dreams and He is still going to fulfill them for you. You are going to see them start to come to pass very soon."

"That's good to hear. I'm about to find out in the next few weeks if I still have my job or not."

"God has great things in store for you because you're very special to Him." He was moving as we spoke, so I could tell he was in a hurry. As I headed down the aisle away from him, I said with a chuckle, "God bless you. When we get to heaven you can let me know what happened with those dreams."

"If I get there," he replied with his own chuckle.

We were now too far apart to say anything, so I just prayed for him. *Lord, if he doesn't yet know You, open his eyes to see how simple it is to be assured of heaven. Help him surrender his life to You and receive Your forgiveness and infilling.*

❧The Preacher❧

So far all of these encounters had been pretty typical for me, but after the recent attacks of the enemy, I felt I was again walking in renewed confidence and expectation. I was once again stepping out in faith, believing that God not only *could,* but *would* speak and work through me. Even so, I asked God for more. *Please give me more details to bless someone today, Lord.* I was excited by what God had done, but hungry for more.

In the cold-food section, I saw a tall gentleman with a little gray in his hair looking around. When I passed by him, the thought "preacher" came to mind. I turned my cart around and boldly asked him, "Are you a preacher of the gospel?"

"Yes, I am," he responded, looking surprised. "How did you know?"

"I was praying for you as I passed by, and the Lord impressed it on my heart."

Faith rose up and I could feel the Holy Spirit working. Rather than trying to figure out what to say, I began speaking and let it flow as if I *were* speaking the very words of God.

"You are a mighty man of God walking in a strong anointing. I sense God all over you." I shared a few more words and the smile grew larger on his face.

His eyes sparkled as he thanked me and explained that he pastors a church that meets in a nearby hotel.

Immediately I saw a picture in my mind's eye and I shared it with him. "I see a picture of you with a leather strap around your chest, and you are pulling a plow behind you. You've had a lot of big rocks and hard ground to plow for many years, and things have been difficult and slow, but the Lord has been blessed by your perseverance and diligence all these years. The Holy Spirit is breaking up the ground for you and things are going to be much easier. You and your church are going to grow exponentially and you're going to see the fruit you have been praying for. God is going to move in power through you, your family and your church."

"That means more to me than you know," he said. "I just preached again for the first time this past Sunday after having been in the hospital for some time."

We chatted briefly about his hospital stay and his church, and the Lord gave more words of encouragement for his heart.

He was apparently familiar with prophecy because he said with a chuckle, "If you're going to prophesy to me, then you need to visit my church."

"I'd be honored!"

We exchanged information and said our good-byes.

My heart was bubbling with joy as I finished up my shopping. *Lord, thank You for once again breaking off the lies of Satan and giving me the confidence to deliver Your love gifts today. No matter how many times I miss it, I'll keep jumping out of the truck and trusting You with the results.*

I wish I could say that was my final faceoff with Satan and doubt, but it wasn't. I am in a battle, and battles are never easy. But the more I ignore my fears and leap out by faith, the easier it becomes to trust God to catch me the next time I leap.

Everyone Misses It at Times

When I do hear incorrectly, I remind myself that even those who have seen the Holy Spirit move through them powerfully still miss it at times. Here are a few examples from the past and present:

PETER

Peter was Jesus' most vocal, passionate, faith-filled disciple who saw numerous healings and miracles, yet he didn't always get things right. He walked on the water until he took his eyes off Jesus and began to sink. On another occasion, he missed hearing God correctly in spite of the fact Jesus was speaking directly to him. Jesus told Peter and the other disciples that He would suffer many things, be rejected, killed and rise again after three days, but Peter took Jesus aside and told Jesus He was wrong and rebuked Him (see Mark 8:31-33). Peter was listening to the lies and fears of the devil rather than Jesus. Peter also said he would die with Jesus rather than deny Him, but before the cock crowed the next morning Peter had denied knowing Jesus three times (see Matthew 26).

After Jesus returned to heaven and the Holy Spirit had been given, we see Peter messing up again in Galatians 2:11-21. He gave into the fear and pressure of legalism and stopped eating with uncircumcised Gentiles. Paul *"opposed him to his face, because he was clearly in the wrong."* Paul saw that Peter was being a hypocrite and leading others astray and *"not acting in line with the truth of the gospel."* He reminded Peter that *"a man is not justified by observing the law, but by faith in Jesus Christ..., for if righteousness could be gained through the law, Christ died for nothing!"*

Although Peter didn't always walk in great faith, hear God correctly or even walk in the truth of the gospel during a short season of legalism, He repented, turned his focus back to God and got back in his GPS truck to share God's love with the world.

PAUL

Paul was another mighty man of God who delivered God's gifts of healings, miracles and prophetic words to countless people. In Acts 21-23 he was in Jerusalem at the temple when a group of Jews stirred up the whole crowd against him. He was arrested and brought to the chief priests and Sanhedrin to find out why he was being accused. *"Paul looked straight at the Sanhedrin and said, 'My brothers, I have fulfilled my duty to God in all good conscience to this day.' At this, the high priest Ananias ordered those standing near Paul to strike him on the mouth. Then Paul said to him, 'God will strike you, you whitewashed wall! You sit there to judge me according to the law, yet you yourself violate the law by commanding that I be struck!"* [The law protected Paul because he was a Roman citizen.] *Those who were standing near Paul said, 'You dare to insult God's high priest?' Paul replied, 'Brothers, I did not realize that he was the high priest; for it is written: Do not speak evil about the ruler of your people'"* (Acts 23:1-5).

When Paul reacted to being struck, he responded out of his flesh rather than listening for the Lord's voice, and as a result, He spoke evil over a Jewish ruler. He immediately realized his mistake and confessed his wrongdoing.

Fortunately for us, the early followers of Jesus weren't perfect. They had to deal with the same challenges in life we do. If they could press forward in spite of their mistakes, so can we.

TODD WHITE

Todd White[11], with Lifestyle Christianity, is a present-day example of sometimes missing it with prophetic words or healing, yet not giving up. Todd was dramatically saved from a life of drug addiction, alcoholism and atheism when God's love flooded his heart. Todd ached for the world to know the amazing God who transformed his life, so he took the Bible at its word and immediately began praying for people everywhere he went. He made it his goal to pray for at least ten people every day—praying for healing and eventually giving prophetic words. As he was faithful to listen and share what he heard, he began to receive more accurate, detailed words from the Lord. After praying for around 1,000 people, he began to see people healed from things like back pain, arthritis, knee and shoulder injuries and various other health issues. His faith had grown as he relentlessly asked God to heal everywhere he went.

Now, only eight years after becoming a Christian, Todd has seen God heal numerous people, especially those he prays for in public. He gives detailed words of knowledge—naming illnesses or pain that God wants to heal, past events in people's lives, or their gifts and talents that God wants to bless and use. He does this in his gentle, loving, non-showy manner wherever he goes, and many people have been saved as a result.

Todd's desire is to reveal God's love in tangible ways just like Jesus did. Some of these interactions are currently on YouTube so you can see God's love in action.

DAN MOHLER

Dan Mohler[12], Todd's spiritual mentor and a tender lover of God, was speaking in our area and I asked him about missing words of knowledge. He himself has delivered many prophetic words and healings, but he said that neither he nor Todd is correct one hundred percent of the time. Dan gave an example from the day before when he asked a lady if she had pain in her shoulder, but she didn't. He said it was as strong a thought as all the other times when he is correct. He did get to minister to her and pray for other areas of need, but his word of knowledge was incorrect.

Dan and Todd's accuracy rates are higher than many, and they see a lot of people healed and touched because they keep taking those leaps of faith and persevering no matter the outcome. But the fact they still miss it at times is an encouragement to the rest of us to keep stepping out by faith even if we pick up the wrong package the first time.

✦Dane's Persistence✦

Another example of prophetic perseverance happened while our family was eating out. We were about to leave the restaurant when I felt a strong impression to bless the family sitting behind us. It was a husband and wife and two small children, so I began by commenting on the children's balloon animals that the balloon artist had given them while they ate. I then shared God's words of love and encouragement with them.

Dane had stopped with me, so after I spoke, he shared what he was feeling for them. "Are you starting a new business?" he asked.

"No," the man responded.

"Are you looking for a new job?"

"No."

"I'm just trying to hear from the Lord," Dane kindly said. "Do either of you have back pain or something wrong with a knee?"

"Yes, I have back problems and a bad knee," the man said.

"Is it your left knee?" Dane asked.

The man nodded *yes*.

"Would you mind if I put a hand on your shoulder and your

knee and pray for them? I've seen a number of shoulders and knees healed."

"Not at all." The man scooted his chair around so Dane could reach his knee.

"Lord, we speak healing in Jesus' name to this back and knee. We command his body to line up with your will and be healed." When Dane finished the prayer he asked, "Do you notice any difference yet?"

The man moved his knee and bent his back. "No. Not that I can tell."

"May I pray again?"

"Sure."

There was still no change after the second prayer.

"We'll keep praying that God will bring His healing power," I piped in. I expected Dane to wrap it up and say good-bye, but he kept asking the Holy Spirit for more.

Dane began to share the gifts, talents and dreams God had given each of them individually and as a couple, and they were both amazed at the accuracy of his words. He shared the ways in which the Lord was going to use those talents and gifts, and fulfill those dreams. I shared a few things I sensed, and before we left I prayed over them, asking God to bless them and to seal and protect what He was doing in their hearts.

If Dane had given up after the first or second mistake, or after the man wasn't healed, this couple would have missed out on tremendous encouragement in those final words of knowledge. The Holy Spirit loves it when we tenaciously keep digging in our truck until we find the right packages—so don't give up!

Chapter Highlights and Application

Verses to Memorize: Put these verses in your phone or post them on your bathroom mirror, and as you memorize them ask the Holy Spirit to keep building your faith. Then let your faith *really* grow by stepping out wherever you're at and speaking God's words of love. You *can* hear God and you *can* speak His words!

> *He who belongs to God hears what God says.*
> **—John 8:47**

> *If anyone speaks, he should do it as one*
> *speaking the very words of God.*
> **—1 Peter 4:11**

It's Okay to Miss it: Missing it or messing up didn't stop Peter or Paul, and it shouldn't stop you or me. If you aren't harboring unforgiveness or walking willingly in sin, then the only thing stopping you from hearing the Holy Spirit is your fear and doubt that He's not speaking. You belong to God, so you can hear what God says. The Holy Spirit told me many years ago that His ability to speak to me is far greater than my inability to hear. Believing that God is eager and able to speak to you isn't arrogance—it's true humility. It's knowing that God is so completely awesome and mighty that your inadequacies are nothing in comparison with His adequacies. It's walking in pure, child-like faith because you know who your Daddy is and what He is capable of accomplishing through you. Keep digging in your truck no matter how many times you miss it, because you have the King of Kings living inside you— speaking *to* you and *through* you.

Chapter 6

Keep it Fun and Stress Free

It's normal to be nervous when you say *No More No* and step into a *Yes, Lord* lifestyle, but you shouldn't be stressed or anxious. Living in the Lord's presence and following His leading wherever you go will be the most amazing journey of your life. Here are twenty-three tips I've discovered along the way to keep it fun and stress free:

TIP #1: LOVE MUST BE YOUR PRIORITY

Paul said to *"eagerly desire spiritual gifts, especially the gift of prophecy"* (1 Corinthians 14:1), but he made it clear that if you operate in the gifts or do any kind deeds without love, you gain nothing (see 1 Corinthians 13:1-3). You are a *"resounding gong or a clanging cymbal"* (13:1). What you say and do is meaningless and irritating if it's not done with love as your highest priority. You'll do more harm than good if you harshly or insensitively give someone a prophetic word or if you pray for their healing in a prideful, condescending attitude.

Even seeing people saved from eternal torment can't be your highest priority. If a person's salvation is your focus rather than love, you'll be tempted to shove salvation truths at someone when the Holy Spirit may be telling you to simply express His love through a prophetic word, a hug or an act of kindness in Jesus' name. The Holy Spirit knows people's hearts and He knows what they need. Your job is to simply ask the Holy Spirit, "How can You and I best love this person and give them what they need to draw them closer to Your heart and truth?"

TIP #2: CHOOSE TO HAVE FUN

Jesus said, *"The thief* [Satan] *comes only to steal and kill and destroy; I came that they may have life, and have it abundantly"* (John 10:10 NASB). When you choose to say *yes* to God's promptings, Satan will come at you from every angle to attack and discourage you. He'll tell you that you're not sharing enough; you're sharing too much; you don't know what you're doing; you should have talked to that person; you shouldn't have talked to that person...and on and on he'll go. Jesus didn't come for you to be bogged down with fear, stress, doubt and guilt. He came so that you could have an abundant life. Walking in the Spirit isn't always easy, but it's fun because you're walking in God's peace and love. If you are feeling stressed with more than the normal fears that you will experience when you first start sharing, recognize what is going on and command Satan and his demons to be silent. Choose to walk in the abundant, joy-filled life Jesus came to give you.

TIP #3: TALK WITH PEOPLE AS IF THEY ARE BELIEVERS

Don't have separate conversations with believers and nonbelievers. Bless family, friends and strangers with glimpses into the goodness of God in your life. Tell them what you read in the Bible that morning or how God used you to share Jesus' love with someone else. Tell them how God provided for a financial need or got you through a recent parenting challenge. Be real and allow the Holy Spirit to guide the conversation. Make people thirsty for more of God in their own lives.

TIP #4: FORGET FORMULAS AND PLANS

Resist the temptation to sneak into manufacturing and create formulas for talking about Jesus. Following formulas will hinder the flow of the Holy Spirit. Even trying to think of salvation scriptures can freeze you up because you'll be focused on inserting them in the conversation rather than focused on listening to the Holy Spirit. The early church in the book of Acts didn't have The Four Spiritual Laws or the Romans Road. They didn't have a New Testament! They simply told people the good news in their own words as the Holy Spirit guided them—and thousands came to Christ. So don't write out your testimony or memorize a speech. Trust the Holy

Spirit and begin talking from your heart. He'll bring to mind helpful Bible verses that you've memorized and meditated on, but don't feel you have to quote Scripture to express God's truth and love. Let it flow.

When the Holy Spirit prompts you to call a relative or friend to express His love, don't plan what you are going to say. (Chances are you'll never get around to it if you feel you have to plan first.) Just say a quick prayer and pick up the phone. You might tell them the Lord prompted you to call to express how much He loves them, and then let the Holy Spirit speak the truth in love through you.

TIP #5: DON'T BE WEIRD OR PREACHY

Okay. I understand weird is a matter of perspective. Giving someone a prophetic word or telling them you sense God's overwhelming love for them is going to be pretty weird. But you don't have to present it weirdly.

Don't speak like a stereotypical TV preacher who talks too loudly and almost sings his sentences, sounding corny and fake. That's a huge turnoff. Be careful, too, not to sound syrupy sweet or drag out your words into a dramatic whisper and come across insincere. Use your normal, friendly voice that you use at home and with friends so that your words and gifts will be well-received.

TIP #6: SLOW DOWN AND LISTEN

Since you'll probably be nervous when you first start sharing gifts with strangers, you'll have a tendency to speed up your voice, share quickly and finish the conversation abruptly. I struggled with this to varying degrees for a long time, so don't kick yourself if you do. Saying something quickly is better than not saying anything at all. But just be aware that your goal is to talk normally and allow for pauses so you can hear what the Holy Spirit is speaking to your thoughts. Don't go overboard and talk so slowly that the person thinks something is wrong with you or wishes you would hurry up and spit it out. Find a good balance.

TIP #7: TALK WITH PEOPLE—NOT AT THEM

A person isn't an emotionless robot to be spoken to as if he or she doesn't have an opinion. Each person you speak with is special beyond compare, with unique thoughts and feelings, so don't talk *at* them, talk *with* them. Whenever possible make your conversation a dialogue, not a speech. Most of the time you'll do the majority of the talking since you are sharing words from the Father's heart, but ask people questions and take time to listen to their responses. Your listening ear may speak as much love to them as the gifts you deliver.

TIP #8: HONOR THE PEOPLE YOU'RE WITH

Your family and friends will have varying comfort levels with a *Yes, Lord* lifestyle, so be sensitive to them when you're in public together until they become more comfortable. If they are completely opposed (especially if it's your spouse), honor them by not sharing with others when you're together or only share when they aren't in earshot. [God will honor you for honoring them, and there is a good chance their hearts will soften and change as they see the fruit of this lifestyle of love.]

If they aren't opposed, but haven't shown interest in engaging in interactions with you, then check with them when you feel impressed to talk with someone and see if they don't mind. Make sure to ask them if they'd like to join in or at least listen and pray during the conversation. I tend to get so focused on who the Lord is highlighting that I forget to touch base and invite those I'm with into the conversation, but I'm working on that.

When you're with younger siblings or your children or grandchildren, make sure to invite them to listen with you and share what they feel the Lord may be saying. Jesus encouraged us to have the faith of a child, so don't shortchange their ability to hear God or their ability to pray in faith. They've had fewer years of listening to the lies of the enemy, which is why their faith is often greater.

When you hang out with someone who also lives a *Yes, Lord* lifestyle, you'll both have different promptings to share with different people, so join each other in ministering God's love when one of you has a prompting. Just be aware of the goal of your outing and the amount of time available. If your goal is to connect with each other and you have limited time together, then you may want to share with others less and interact with each other more. If you are at the grocery store or running errands, and not necessarily in need of connecting, then sharing with more people will work well. The Holy Spirit knows all the issues at hand, so He'll lovingly work with what's happening.

TIP # 9: REMEMBER THIS IS A LIFESTYLE

Planning a time to go out with one or two people with the specific goal of saying *yes* to God's promptings can be helpful, encouraging and extremely fruitful. I would highly encourage you to do this if the Lord is leading you in that direction.

My only caution is that you don't get in the mindset that listening to the Holy Spirit is an event—something you do when it's scheduled. Listening and responding to the Holy Spirit's voice is a lifestyle. It's like breathing in and out. It never stops. Your goal is to be in constant communication with the Father and to say *yes* in everything He asks you to do—at home, in your neighborhood, at school, at work, at the grocery store and wherever you go.

TIP #10: GIVE YOURSELF EXTRA TIME

Since you are listening to the Holy Spirit wherever you go, make a point to give yourself extra time when you go places. It doesn't necessarily take long to stop and talk with people, but if you aren't feeling rushed, then you'll be more inclined to listen to the Holy Spirit. Leave for work, school, the store or meetings earlier than necessary to have more time to share from the Lord's heart if He prompts you.

Even if you are in a hurry, don't forget that God can express His love in less than a minute. Stay open to what He is doing in the people around you. Sometimes your being late will actually be God's way of connecting you with someone. God is incredibly intelligent and when you allow Him to lead you, you'll be amazed at how He'll guide you to people at the perfect time.

TIP #11: BE PREPARED FOR THE BACK-TO-BACK

Sometimes God will prompt you to speak with one person and then immediately prompt you to speak with another. This can feel uncomfortable if the first person can still see or hear you. I don't want people to feel like they are a project and that I'm just talking indiscriminately to everyone I see, and I'm afraid that's what they'll think. But I have to trust that God will guard their hearts and go ahead and obey even if they are back-to-back promptings.

TIP #12: BE POLITE AND SENSITIVE TO YOUR SURROUNDINGS

When Buddy from the movie *Elf* first discovered real-people toilets were bigger than the elf toilets he grew up with, he stood on the toilet seat, looked over into the next stall and expressed his excitement to the guy beside him. It was hilarious in the movie, but obviously inappropriate and insensitive in real life. In your excitement to share God's love gifts with the world, aim to be as polite and sensitive as possible. Make honoring people a priority.

As much as your heart wants to tell the whole world of God's love, pray for wisdom and discernment. God may ask you to share in crazy ways, but He won't ask you to do it insensitively. God doesn't force Himself rudely on us, so we shouldn't force ourselves rudely on others. I often stop and share for a few minutes with people as I'm walking in or out of a restaurant, but I wouldn't stand up on my chair in the middle of the restaurant and share with everyone. No matter how loving my words were, it would dishonor the owner's desire for a peaceful atmosphere and it would irritate the patrons. Interrupting every conversation in a restaurant and forcing everyone to listen to you would express a lack of concern for them as individuals.

There may be other public settings where the Holy Spirit prompts you to share something with the whole crowd where listening is optional and they can choose to stay or leave—like at a park—so be open to this possibility. God may just bring open-air meetings back into popularity through you.

TIP #13: REJECTION ISN'T ABOUT YOU (unless you ignored the previous tips)

I have seen people do some really harsh, unkind things in the name of sharing Jesus, and it's no surprise people reject them. You've probably seen them, too: People holding "Turn or Burn" signs or handing out angry-sounding tracts that talk about the wrath of God if they don't repent. Yes, we all need to repent and turn from our sin, but why would anyone want to spend an eternity in heaven with a God they feel is only full of anger and wrath? I wouldn't. We need to introduce people to the God who loves them like crazy and then tell them how they can be forgiven and spend eternity living with Him in that incredible love.

If you are walking in love and presenting Jesus' gifts with honor and respect, and someone rejects what you are saying, don't take it personally. Jesus said in Luke 10:16: *"He who listens to you listens to me; he who rejects you rejects me; but he who rejects me rejects him who sent me."* So when they reject your message of truth or your gift of love, they aren't rejecting you, but Jesus. And if they reject Jesus, they are rejecting the Father because Jesus said, *"I and the Father are one"* (John 10:30).

Jesus said when you are hated, excluded, insulted and rejected because of Him to *"Rejoice in that day and leap for joy, because great is your reward in heaven"* (see Luke 6:22-23). If you have lovingly and sensitively shared what the Holy Spirit prompted you to say or do, and someone responds rudely or makes fun of you, go dance a little jig. You may get spit at here on earth, but you are blessing all of heaven with your boldness and love.

All that being said, in the past three-and-a-half years of saying *yes* to the Holy Spirit's promptings, I've only had two extremely angry reactions to my sharing God's love and forgiveness (and both of those were relatives) and less than fifteen disinterested or mildly irritated reactions from family, friends or strangers. If you are saying *yes* to God's promptings and experiencing a lot of negative reactions, humbly ask the Holy Spirit to show you if your presentation of God's gifts comes across judgmental, proud or rude. I'm often upfront with family, friends or strangers about the importance of receiving Jesus' forgiveness or about issues that are somewhat corrective, but my prayer is that every word I speak is bathed in the Father's love and gentleness. I'm not perfect, and I know I've irritated people, but because they feel my love for them they usually don't attack me. This will change as wickedness increases on the earth, but for now, this is what I'm experiencing and seeing others experience who live this same lifestyle in love.

TIP #14: GOD USES IMPERFECT PEOPLE

Jesus said to, *"Be perfect, therefore, as your heavenly Father is perfect"* (Matthew 5:48), but He also said, *"The spirit is willing, but the flesh is weak"* (Matthew 26:41). Our weakness is no surprise to Jesus. He was here. He understands the battle and He understands that becoming more perfect in love is a process as we draw nearer to His heart. As I previously mentioned, Paul was a phenomenal GPS delivery man who delivered miracles, healings and deep spiritual revelations, but he made a point to mention his struggle with sin in Romans 7:15: *"For what I want to do I do not do, but what I hate I do."* Paul wasn't perfect, but God used him because he was willing to say *yes* in spite of his weaknesses.

I'm far from perfect, but the Holy Spirit still graciously uses me in delivery. Here's the short list of my issues (see my family for the long list):

- I get irritated sometimes by marriage or parenting challenges and get snippy
- I like sugar and junk, so I have to keep it out of the house
- I love to organize and plan—my life and others'
- I sometimes fail to persevere and stick with my plans
- I stay up too late at night far too often (especially when I'm working on projects)
- I battle my desire to watch DVDs rather than read or be productive

I've seen huge improvements in each of these areas over the years because several of them were serious addictions or issues, but I still need God's love working in my heart and changing me on a daily basis. Getting frustrated with a family member, overeating junk food or watching too many movies doesn't disqualify me from blessing someone with a gift from God, but it does mean I need to apologize when necessary and continue to fix my eyes on Jesus instead of food and entertainment. The issues that you battle don't disqualify you from sharing God's love and gifts either. If you're in the midst of battling addictions, depression, anger or other sins, God still wants to use you. When you blow it, don't beat yourself up. Thank Jesus for the forgiveness you received when you became a believer; ask others to forgive you and accept God's grace to go forward, asking for strength to do better the next time.

Satan wants us filled with guilt so we feel unworthy to share God's love, but Jesus paid the price so that you and I could be made worthy and totally free from all accusation. *"But now He has reconciled you by Christ's physical body through death to present you holy in His sight, without blemish and free from accusation—if you continue in your faith, established and firm...."* (Colossians 1:22-23). We are free from accusation and have been made worthy—not only to be in the Lord's presence, but to be His mouthpiece, His hands and His feet.

TIP #15: GOD KNOWS WHAT YOU DON'T KNOW

You don't have to be a Bible scholar to share God's love. God knows what you know and what you don't know, so He'll direct you to the right people and give you the words to say. Jesus said, *"At that time you will be given what to say, for it will not be you speaking, but the Spirit of your Father speaking through you"* (Matthew 10:19-20).

This doesn't mean you should stop learning. God will reveal fresh truths daily as you talk with Him, read the Bible and become involved in a good church. The more you have stored up in your heart, the more you'll have to give. But don't be overwhelmed and feel you need to know everything about everything. The Holy Spirit will give you the words to say.

Even when talking with people who are part of another religion, don't worry if you don't know the details of their religion. Just share the joy that came when you were freed from rules and regulations into a relationship with Jesus. That is the one thing that sets Christianity apart from all other religions. Christians don't have to fulfill a list of dos and don'ts because when Jesus died for us He said it was done—it was finished.

TIP #16: THESE ARE GIFTS—NOT REWARDS

The reason a new believer can immediately begin operating in the gifts of the Spirit is because they are gifts. They aren't given based on our level of spiritual maturity or knowledge. Just as salvation can't be earned, the gifts of the Spirit can't be earned. Being able to give encouraging words of prophecy or pray for the sick and see people healed are gifts. If we think we have to earn them, then we'll never have them. Jesus told His disciples, *"Heal the sick, raise the dead, cleanse those who have leprosy, drive out demons. Freely you have received, freely give"* (Matthew 10:8). The gifts are free. Our only job is to break off the lies of the enemy telling us we can't have them, and then step out by faith and freely pass them out.

After the crippled beggar was healed, Peter asked the people, *"Why do you stare at us as if by our own power or godliness we had made this man walk?"* (Acts 3:12). Peter knew it wasn't his own power that healed the man and it wasn't a result of his godliness. It was God's power activated by Peter's faith.

TIP #17: YOU CAN'T DELIVER TO EVERYONE

Satan will try to discourage you by making you feel guilty for the people you *aren't* talking to, but you are only one person just as Jesus was only one person, limited by being in a physical body. Jesus knew His time was short on the earth and He couldn't minister to everyone, so He made it clear *"I was sent only to the lost sheep of Israel"* (Matthew 15:24). His job was to preach to the Jews, knowing that He would later send His disciples out to preach to the whole world.

Jesus wasn't stressed by the people He couldn't reach because He trusted the Father's leading. He said, *"I tell you the truth, the Son can do nothing by Himself; He can do only what He sees His Father doing, because whatever the Father does the Son also does. For the Father loves the Son and shows Him all He does"* (John 5:19-20). The Father loves you, too, and will lead you just as He led the Son, so relax and trust Him to direct your path.

TIP #18: ALLOW YOURSELF BAD DAYS

There will be days when the last thing you'll want to do is strike up a conversation with someone. That's okay and the Holy Spirit understands, but rather than shut Him down, talk with Him about it. I often tell Him, "Holy Spirit, I'm tired (or grumpy or feeling hurt) and don't have the slightest inkling to share Your love, but I'm here and I trust Your love for me. Change my attitude if there is someone You want me to bless for You." I may not share with anyone, and I believe the Holy Spirit is totally fine with that, but more often than not, He'll change my heart as I shop. I've had some very powerful encounters on my tired, grumpy or wounded days, and it's amazing how my spirits are lifted once I do.

TIP #19: *DON'T STRESS OVER THE OUTCOME*

Your job is to deliver gifts of love. You're not responsible for people's reactions to those gifts or what they do with the gifts. A UPS employee doesn't come into your house when he drops off a package to make sure you use what's in the package. He delivers it and leaves the use of the package up to you.

As a GPS employee, you get to do the same. Once you have expressed the Father's love, given a word, prayed for someone or shared the good news of Jesus' forgiveness, you get to leave the outcome in the Holy Spirit's hands. He will continue to work and move in their hearts as He's been doing their whole lives.

TIP #20: *NOT EVERYONE IS READY*

Not everyone is ready to receive Christ's love and forgiveness, so let go of the pressure to seal the deal, and simply share what the Holy Spirit places on your heart. Certainly be willing to pray with people to receive Christ if the Lord takes the conversation that way and you sense they are ready. But be careful not to push someone to pray when they aren't truly ready to submit their life to God's leadership because this could do more harm than good in the long run. They will be left with a false sense of security if they think it's about saying the right words rather than about the position of their heart. Being a believer isn't about signing up for fire insurance to obtain a *Get Out of Hell Free* pass. Being a believer is about believing.

This isn't to say someone must have everything figured out before they ask Jesus to forgive them. God will grow their understanding once He comes to live inside them. I was only seven when I received Christ, and all I knew was that I did bad things and that I needed to be forgiven. I wanted God to live inside me and be with me all the time.

The criminal crucified beside Jesus on the cross only knew that Jesus was from God and had done nothing wrong. As he hung there dying, with only minutes left to live, he believed. *"Jesus, remember me when you come into your kingdom."* Jesus told him, *"Today you will be with me in paradise"* (Luke 23:42-43).

Trust the Holy Spirit to show you if someone is ready to receive Jesus as their Lord and Savior.

TIP #21: RELEASE THE BURDEN

Sadly, Satan will try to weigh you down with the burden that you are responsible for the salvation of every person you know and encounter. He uses this lie to discourage and depress believers. Jesus was the first employee and the only perfect employee for God's Parcel Service, but He didn't lead everyone into a right relationship with God.

When Satan tries to stress you with the fact that people you share with and people you know are not yet believers, choose to release the burden and leave it in the Lord's hands where it belongs. Your part is simply to do your part—nothing more, nothing less. You need to pray when the Holy Spirit prompts you to pray and share when the Holy Spirit prompts you to share. You can't take on the responsibility of feeling you have to pray people into heaven or talk people into heaven, because it can't be done. That's God's job. Jesus said, *"No one can come to me unless the Father who sent me draws him"* (John 6:44). He is constantly drawing everyone to His heart, so trust God to keep working and moving in their lives.

TIP #22: TRUST GOD WITH THE FOLLOW-UP

If you do have the privilege of leading someone into a relationship with Jesus, don't stress about the follow-up. Just as the Holy Spirit led you to that person and guided the conversation, He'll lead you in how to help them grow in their new walk with God. He may lead you to be extremely involved in their lives as they begin to read the Bible, learn to talk constantly with God and discover the importance of being around other Christians in church or Bible studies. But there is a good chance God will use others to help that person grow, so don't feel their growth will rest on your shoulders.

If I pray with someone to receive Jesus' forgiveness, I make sure to get their phone number and I give them mine. Normally I give my phone number out when I talk with people, but I don't take people's numbers because it puts too much pressure on me to feel I need to call everyone. This way, if they want to call me they can. But when someone is a new believer, I make sure to contact them, give them a Bible and try to get them plugged into a church if possible. Some people will be eager to grow and become part of a church and others won't. I have to trust the Holy Spirit to keep working in their lives and not allow their growth to become my burden. I simply pray for them and trust the Holy Spirit to lead me in my interactions with them.

Even with all the people I've talked to and prayed with, the Lord has never overwhelmed me with too much to do or too many people to help. People seem to come in and out of my life as God leads. (I've only had to purposely back off of one relationship because that person was not treating me and my time with kindness.)

TIP #23: RECORD AND SHARE YOUR STORIES

Keep a journal of what God is doing in and through you as you say *yes* to His promptings. Reading your stories will encourage you when the enemy lies and says you aren't making a difference. You *are* making a difference one person at a time!

Other people will be encouraged by your *Yes, Lord* stories, so tell them your stories when the Holy Spirit prompts you to. Be aware there will be times when He'll prompt you *not* to share because you could be sharing out of pride or your sharing could discourage the listener rather than encourage them. As in everything, stay sensitive to the Father's leading and obey His promptings.

Chapter Highlights and Application

The "Yes, Lord" Lifestyle is Fun: If you aren't having fun as you listen to the Holy Spirit and share His love gifts, then the devil is messing with your head. Silence his lies and enjoy doing life with the God of the universe who is living inside you. God created you for love—to receive His love and to give His love back to Him and to His world. Nothing is more fun than that!

The "Yes, Lord" Lifestyle is Stress Free: Stress and worry about what to say or do—or not to say or do—are the devil's tools to keep you silent. Choose daily to trust God's love and leading in your life. Usually the worst that happens when you step out of the GPS truck is you feel or look a little foolish or uncomfortable. Western Christians are not currently being heavily persecuted for their faith if they share with the kindness of Jesus, but even if that changes, Jesus said in Mark 13:11, *"Whenever you are arrested and brought to trial, do not worry beforehand about what to say. Just say whatever is given you at the time, for it is not you speaking, but the Holy Spirit."* No matter the circumstances or where you are (even on trial for your faith), you don't have to stress or worry about what to say because the Holy Spirit will give you the words. You can relax and trust God's love and His ability to speak through you!

Part 3

Stories to Inspire

Chapters 7 and 8 are stories from one month of my life as I said *yes* to God's promptings. They allow you to see what this lifestyle looks like for me at this point in my journey. Chapter 9 features stories from other radicals who are also saying *yes* to God's leading in their lives.

Feel free to read these next three chapters all at once or intermix them with reading the final three chapters of the book. (The final three chapters teach powerful and practical truths for breaking free from fear and apathy.)

Chapter 7

March Boldly—A Month of Encounters

⊱Crazy Lady in the Theatre⊰

I settled into the theatre's side aisle seat beside Ron, disappointed we hadn't arrived sooner and been able to sit in the center of the middle section to enjoy the best surround-sound effect. We rarely find movies that don't take God's name in vain or have cussing or sexual content, so it's a treat when there is a clean film we can enjoy in the theatre. I looked around as the seats continued to fill and realized I'd gladly sit on the floor to make more room because this film, *Son of God,* was about Jesus.

Throughout the movie I had the privilege of talking with the star of the show while I watched the film about His life. What a perk! I asked Him to work in the hearts of everyone in the theatre and everyone who would watch this movie. *Jesus, open their hearts to Your incredible love and forgiveness.* I prayed for more of Jesus in my own life. *Fill me to overflowing with all the love, wisdom and power You walked in on the earth. You said it is available for me, so help me receive it.* I prayed for increased faith. *Help me daily step out on the water like Peter and trust You completely.*

Three-fourths of the way through the film, Jesus gave me the chance to step out on the water right then and there. His words burst into my thoughts: *"Stand up at the end of the movie and share My love."* My whole body shook and my heart began to race.

I have no doubt this is You speaking, Lord, but wow, this is a big one for me! There is nothing in my flesh that wants to stand up in front of at least 300 people, but I choose to fix my eyes on You and Your love, and not on the people or circumstances around me. The worse that can happen is I'll look like a fool.

Ron isn't wild about this kind of thing, so I'll quickly leave my seat and stand in the front so it won't make him uncomfortable. That way I can honor both You and Ron at the same time. This must be why You directed us to an aisle seat. You're so smart. Please give me the words to say....

I prayed fervently, missing parts of the movie because I was so intent. The Lord showed me that many people in the theatre were Christians, but there were some whose hearts were burning because they now believed in Jesus and wanted to be saved. There were also Christians who hadn't been walking closely with the Lord or walking in obedience to His promptings in their lives. I felt Him telling me to address both.

I didn't tell Ron because I didn't want to stress him. When the movie was drawing to a close I was shaking, so I leaned over and whispered in Ron's ear, "Pray for me." Fortunately, he didn't ask why.

The movie concluded with Jesus telling His disciples to go into all the world and preach the gospel. It was the perfect segue. As soon as the first credits appeared on the screen I stood up and began speaking as I quickly walked to the front. Unfortunately, I had to almost shout to be heard over the film's music.

"Please don't leave yet. I told the Lord almost three years ago I would no longer say *no* when He prompted me to say something, and the Lord prompted me to speak." I made it to the front and turned fully around. "There are those of you whose hearts are burning because you now believe and want to receive Jesus' forgiveness. He loves you and wants you to stand and receive Him into your life to fill you with His love and walk with you through life. There are also those of you who are believers, but haven't been walking with the Lord closely or walking in the boldness you desire. If you want to receive Jesus into your life or if you want to walk in boldness and obedience, then please stand and pray with me." Many people in the theatre stood up—whether to pray or to leave, I don't know—because I immediately closed my eyes, raised my hands and began praying, still almost shouting to be heard.

"Jesus, we thank You for Your love. Come forgive us and fill us with Your presence. We need You, Lord. You came to earth to die for our sins because You love us like crazy. Help us walk in Your love and power. Help us say *yes* to You wherever we go, whether at the grocery store, work or school. Break off all fear of man so that we can follow Your promptings. Make us bold and transform McKinney and the surrounding area through us. McKinney needs You, Jesus. Move in power in our city. Thank You for Your love. We love You so much. Amen."

It wasn't eloquent, but it was from my heart. A sweet lady standing behind me was a big encouragement by loudly praying, "Yes, Lord" and "Amen, Jesus" as I prayed. When I opened my eyes, the theatre was less full, but there were still people standing with me. Several people thanked me as they headed out, including the lady behind me. I turned to give her a hug and we spoke for a few moments.

When I turned back around, a twelve-year-old young man was standing in front of me with his dad beside him. The young man looked at me and didn't say anything, so I asked, "Would you like to ask Jesus to forgive you and live inside you?"

"Yes," he said.

"What is your name?"

"Tommy" (not his real name).

"My name is Julie," I shook his hand. "Tommy, God has amazing things for you. How incredible that you have the boldness to receive Jesus in a theatre—in a public place. God is going to use you publicly as a mighty warrior and as His mouthpiece. I see a picture in my mind's eye of you in armor and as a powerful warrior of love for Jesus. God is going to show you and your family His gifts that will equip you to do His work on the earth!" He looked intently at me, not sure what to make of all this.

I asked his dad if he also wanted to receive Jesus, but he said he already had, so I turned back to Tommy. "If you want to be forgiven and live for Jesus, then repeat this prayer after me." (I didn't have a prayer memorized. I just let it flow.)

"Jesus, please forgive me of all my sins.

"My past, present and future sins.

"Come live inside me and lead my life...."

We continued to pray together, asking the Holy Spirit to fill Tommy with His love and power so that he could boldly share God's love with his world.

When we finished, I gave him a big hug and explained that God and the angels were rejoicing over the fact he will spend eternity with them. I talked with Tommy and his dad as the theatre employees were cleaning around us, and we continued to talk as we walked outside. His dad told me they attended a Catholic church and were interested in learning more about the Holy Spirit. God had been stirring things of the Spirit from a number of angles in his life. We talked for over twenty minutes and then exchanged phone numbers and said good-bye with one final hug of congratulations to Tommy.

As Ron and I got in the car, it was obvious Ron was irritated, so I asked him what his thoughts were. He felt the whole experience was awkward and felt chaotic since I had to shout to be heard. He said most people couldn't hear what I was saying in the back. One gentleman near him had acted irritated and said something about me being crazy as he walked out. While people in the front could hear and were responding, Ron felt it may have done more harm than good for those in the back.

I agreed that the circumstances were not ideal and the noise made it chaotic, but I knew if I hadn't obeyed, I would have regretted it forever. And if I hadn't obeyed, one young man would have missed the chance to boldly come forward in a theatre to receive Christ.

☙Brother Returns to Christ in the Pen❧

After leaving the theatre, Ron and I stopped by a nearby grocery store to grab some steak for what I had hoped would be a romantic supper. Last month, February 2014, Sierra had moved out on her own, so Dane was the only one still living with us while he attended college. He spent the weekend at his grandparents so Ron and I could stay in the "Earl Resort" for the weekend.

As we walked into the grocery store, the Holy Spirit highlighted a lady we passed. I knew it was bad timing to stop, so I prayed for her. Ron and I found a good deal on steak and headed to the check-out. When we got in line, I noticed that same lady was checking out beside us. Since Ron was busy paying, I decided to speak with her.

I stepped up behind her and her family. "Hi!" I said enthusiastically with a smile. When I passed you a few minutes ago, the Lord impressed you on me."

"Who?"

"The Lord. I felt God's overwhelming love for you and your family, and that He wanted to remind you of that love."

I found out later in the conversation that it was her mother and niece who were with her. Her mother quickly jumped in. "We're actually visiting a church tomorrow because my son asked if we would."

"That's great! Which church are you going to?" She told me the name of the church and we talked about it since I had visited there several years ago and had been impressed.

The daughter added, "We're actually going because my brother just got out of the pen four days ago and he asked if we could go to church together."

"Did he become a Christian while he was in jail?" I asked.

"He came back around," the mother said. We talked about this a little longer and then I felt the Holy Spirit wanted to encourage her son.

"Please tell your son that God has his number. He knows everything about him and loves him deeply. He is on the right path and God has good things in store for him."

"Thank you. I will," she said. Ron had just finished checking out so I said good-bye. I felt this simple encounter was no accident. It was God's way of encouraging a man newly released from prison that He would lead him on the *outside* just as He led him on the *inside*.

MARCH BOLDLY

After Ron and I ate our steak and had a calm, but unpleasant discussion about the theatre event and a few other things, I went for a walk in our neighborhood even though it was already dark. I was feeling hurt and needed to pray and process Ron's embarrassment and his frustration with me.

As I walked, the Holy Spirit comforted me with His love by sweetly singing to my thoughts, *"I love you a bushel and a peck. A bushel and a peck and a hug around the neck…."* I sang it back to Him and chuckled at His thoughtfulness. This is the song I have sung many times to my kids, and now to my grandson. The Holy Spirit's peace settled over me, and my heart began to heal.

The Lord encouraged me to keep my heart soft and not allow a wall to go up between Ron and me even if we never see eye to eye in this. I had lived too many seasons with some sort of wall to protect myself—where I was a good wife, but not loving with all my heart. I've learned that my job is to keep my heart tender and loving—holding nothing back—and the Comforter's job is to keep my heart protected from more than it can handle, and to heal my heart when it's wounded.

I continued talking with the Lord about what had happened at the theatre. Should I have done something differently? Should I have asked people to come to the front if they needed prayer rather than almost yelling over the noise? That certainly was an option, but I felt in that moment, and I felt again as I walked and prayed, that God wanted more from me. He had drawn a line in the sand and asked me to make a choice: To stay behind the line where it was safe or to cross the line and step into new levels of faith, risk and obedience.

Sadly, I may have irritated some people and turned them off, but I can't let the fear of what people think be my guide. If I'm positive it's the Holy Spirit's voice, I can't stop and weigh the pros and cons. I have to trust He has already considered the outcome and He knows what is best for all concerned in the long run. Perhaps those people who left the theatre thinking I was crazy may never forget what I said. God may remind them of my words when their hearts are soft and ready to receive. Or if they're already Christians, they may be more willing to stand up and say *yes* to the Holy Spirit when He asks them to do something scary or crazy.

I do know a shift took place in my heart when I stepped out onto the "water" in that theatre. Another layer of fear fell away.

I finished my walk and sat on our front porch bench. The Holy Spirit continued to speak to my heart:

"It's no coincidence, Julie, that this all happened on March 1ˢᵗ. I am giving you marching orders to step into that new level of risk and fruit you have been asking for. You will MARCH BOLDLY in My will. You will take risks you've never taken, and I will bless you for your obedience. Write down what happens this month and place it in your book—the mess-ups and the victories, the good and the bad. Trust Me and enjoy the wild ride because I love you, dear one!"

Thank You, Holy Spirit, for Your tender love and for healing my heart when Ron and I don't see eye to eye. I love You so much, and I am honored to say yes to Your promptings and march boldly with You in whatever You ask me to do. I'll gladly write down what happens this month and see how You work in and through me

SUNDAY, MARCH 2ⁿᵈ

I was home working today and didn't interact with anyone, so I'll take this opportunity to share some fun news. Ron and the Holy Spirit gave the green light last month to move forward with Crazy About You Ministries (CAYM). Starting this ministry has been on my heart for many years, so I couldn't be more excited to be a part of what God is going to do through CAYM (pronounced "came"). Preparing to launch CAYM will take up a great deal of my time this month, so for brevity's sake, I'll only record my *Yes, Lord* encounters as I interact with people, not all the other activities bustling behind the scenes.

Since this is the birthing of a life-long dream to share Jesus with my world and equip others to do the same, allow me to share a sneak peek into CAYM's current mission statement and how I believe that mission will be accomplished:

Crazy About You Ministries (CAYM)
Jesus CAYM because He's crazy about you!
Experience God's Love…Express God's Love

CAYM's mission is to help people experience God's incredible, life-changing love and forgiveness, and teach believers to daily express that love by listening to the Holy Spirit and saying yes to His promptings.

This will be accomplished through powerful online video testimonies of God's transforming love; online studies and blogs for seekers and believers; phone and email prayer support; this book, *No More No,* and the coinciding Bible study for small group and personal study; conferences, retreats and speaking engagements for CAYM speakers; local outreaches and short-term overseas mission trips to share God's love and to put the *Yes, Lord* lifestyle into action.

Can you tell I'm a little excited? This, too, is another opportunity to step out on the water and see God work miracles. Fortunately for me, the Holy Spirit is the real founding president and CEO, and He has promised to work out every detail as I stay in His presence, walk in His love and peace, and simply do what He asks each day. I love that business plan!

MONDAY, MARCH 3rd

The Internet is a fantastic way to express God's love. Since Facebook is still one of the current trends, I quickly check my wall and groups several times a day. When I'm on Facebook, I look for opportunities to be a blessing by sharing words of encouragement whenever possible. If someone is having a birthday, I try to write a kind comment about their character. If I have more time, I'll ask the Holy Spirit for a short prophetic word to encourage them.

Today there were two ladies celebrating their birthdays, and I was able to take a little extra time to listen for words from the Holy Spirit. I received a picture and the meaning for one of the ladies, and for the other young lady I had a word about the calling on her life. The words were short and simple, but both of them seemed to be blessed, so it was worth the extra time.

TUESDAY, MARCH 4th

❧Email Plunge❧

I signed up to work at a nearby grocery store handing out flour tortilla samples for a company promoting their product. A man I'll call Jack, who works for the staffing agency, was in charge of this particular event, so he had been emailing me information. I felt prompted to prophesy words of encouragement for Jack through email this morning, so after a few emails back and forth about the upcoming job, I took the plunge, praying for guidance:

Jack, on a totally random note, I am trying to hear from the Lord more clearly for other people. God is always speaking His thoughts for me, but I want to get to where I can hear better what he is speaking for people around me. The Bible calls it a word of knowledge when you are given something from the Lord you wouldn't know on your own. If you don't mind, I'd like to try to hear from Him for you. You can stop reading now if you think I'm crazy. LOL

Here goes. Please feel free to let me know what I miss and if I get anything right. My heart is to bless people, and I can't get better if I don't take risks and try to hear. Thanks for your kindness and patience!

Jack, I picture you as a strong, dark-haired gentleman. I see you interacting quite a bit with two women—maybe sisters—especially when you were younger. You went to a Catholic church growing up and there is still a soft place in your heart for God. Your relationship with your father wasn't what you always wanted, but your mother spoke many things into your life. You have a grateful heart in many areas, but you want more for your life—more success in business and in relationships.

You are a man of character, and doing what is right is important to you. You have tremendous leadership ability. It is a challenge for you to follow through, but you are doing it and seeing results. You are a man of your word and it bothers you greatly when you or others don't keep their word. You like animals, especially dogs, because you have the gift of nurturing and you enjoy the strength dogs represent. You like to stay in shape, but it's hard to do with your busy schedule.

I don't know if I got any of that right, but I am really feeling the Lord's love for you right now as I pray blessings over you. I sense there is a powerful calling on your life to dig deep into your relationship with the Lord so that others will be able to eat the "crop" that you dig up. Many will find healing and sustenance from the truths God reveals as you draw closer to the Father's heart.

I see you going against the flow of society and calling others to go against that flow. I am picturing you in a river standing firm as the water swirls around you and people glide past you. You are gently grabbing on to many people and setting them on the shore in a place of safety and rest until they are strong enough in their relationship with Jesus to join you in your rescue efforts.

You are very loved by the Father. He knows everything about you and His thoughts are continually toward you. The Bible says your name is written in the palm of His hand. Now that's love!

Thanks for allowing me to jump in the water and take this risk. I pray even if I am wrong in some of my impressions, that the Lord will wash His love over you today and every day. You are extremely special to Him!!

Many blessings and have a great day!
Julie

I wish I could report that this word was correct and Jack responded with enthusiasm, but as it turned out, Jack didn't respond at all. He sent me a couple emails about the job, but he never mentioned my attempt to hear from the Holy Spirit. It made me wonder: Was Jack actually a blond dog-hater who had never set foot in a Catholic church, and I was so far off that he didn't want to embarrass me? That thought made me chuckle, because perhaps he was being silent out of kindness. Another option was that the word hit too close to home, and he wasn't ready to deal with what was spoken. No matter the real reason for Jack's silence, I know the Lord loves Jack with a love I can't comprehend, and the Lord will continue to love Jack relentlessly.

As for me, more fear dissolved as I risked such a specific word. I sensed Jesus' pleasure in the fact that I again stepped out of the boat. Even if I later find out the prophetic word was inaccurate, I felt my faith honored Jesus, and Jesus would in turn honor my faith.

❧Costco Encounters❧

After an encouraging and helpful mid-morning meeting with my writer's critique group, I drove to Costco to buy some specialty and organic groceries for our currently gluten-free, dairy-free, pesticide-free, sugar-free, junk-free diet.

When I arrived, I prayed as I grabbed a cart and headed in. *Lord, here I am. Have Your way and allow me to express Your love at Costco.* I prayed for people, but I didn't feel led to stop until I saw an older gentleman in a boot cast.

"That looks uncomfortable. How did you hurt yourself?"

He told me the story. "It actually doesn't hurt at the moment, but I have to be in this boot for four more weeks.

"Is it okay if I pray for you?" I asked.

"Sure," he responded, a little surprised.

I put my hand on his shoulder and closed my eyes since he had closed his. "Lord, thank you for this amazing man. I ask in Jesus' name that you would heal his ankle and make it stronger than it's ever been. Bring complete restoration. You love him and know everything about him. Bless all that he does and allow him to feel your arms around him. Bless his family and every part of his life...." I prayed a few more sentences and then said, "Amen."

"Thank you," he said with a gentle smile.

"You're welcome. Do you go to a church around here?"

He proceeded to tell me about his church that he occasionally attended, and we talked for several more minutes before we said good-bye and I headed down the aisle.

When I turned the corner to the next aisle, a pretty middle-aged lady was shopping with her four-year-old granddaughter in the cart. The little girl had on sparkly pink shoes.

"Wow! Those are beautiful shoes!" I exclaimed.

"Thank you," the little girl shyly responded. I chatted with both of them for a minute. *Do you have anything for them, Holy Spirit?* The thought came to mind that there was something wrong in one of the grandmother's relationships.

"I was just asking the Lord to bless you, and I sensed there were some challenges in a relationship. Does that make any sense?"

"Well, I can't think of anything." She thought for a few seconds. "My dog just died yesterday, though, so that may be what you're talking about. My dog was a very special friend to me and I miss him terribly." We talked a little longer about her dog and how much he meant to the whole family.

"I'm so sorry for your loss. Pets are important family members." I put my hand on her shoulder, and with my eyes still open, I prayed, "Lord, bring your healing to this precious lady and her whole family." When I finished my one-sentence prayer, I sensed a few things for her, so I quickly shared them before we said our good-byes.

I was short on time, so I didn't talk to as many people as I would have liked, but I prayed God's love would bless the people I passed. I never want to underestimate the power of prayer because God chooses to work through our prayers. When we pray, things shift in the spirit realm. James 5:16 says, *"The prayer of a righteous man is powerful and effective."* We don't always see the results immediately in the physical realm, but the weapons we fight with—God's truth, our prayers and our acts of faith—demolish demonic strongholds and lies that people are believing (see 2 Corinthians 10:3-5).

Even though I was pulling down strongholds as I zipped through the store, the thoughts started to come: *You should stop and talk with more people. You're not being very spiritual. How can you write about this and teach others when you don't share all the time?* After a few moments, I realized this was demonic.

Be silent, demonic liars. "There is now no condemnation for those who are in Christ Jesus" (Romans 8:1). *The Holy Spirit works through loving conviction—not judgment. I command you to be silent, and I choose to enjoy my day!* The guilt and discouraging thoughts ceased, and I enjoyed the rest of my shopping, sharing friendly chatter with several people and the cashier.

WEDNESDAY, MARCH 6th

✥Chasing the Cane✥

I was waiting in the large, tastefully-decorated lobby of The Hope Center. This 185,000 square foot facility had been built because of a vision given to June Hunt to support Christian ministries by providing low-cost office space and other resources to help them spread the good news about Jesus around the world. The building currently rents space to over forty different ministries.

I had come to speak with two ladies from one of those ministries, but they were apparently tied up in a meeting. A few moments after sitting down to wait, I noticed a man with a cane step out of the elevator and hobble toward the front doors. The thought flashed in my mind to pray for him, but I was afraid one of the ladies might arrive any minute. After a forty-five second struggle, I told the Lord *yes* and trusted Him to work it out.

By this time the man was outside, so I had to chase him out to the parking lot. *I bet this looks suspicious,* I thought. "Excuse me, sir!" I half shouted to get his attention. When he saw I was calling him, he turned around and hobbled back onto the sidewalk.

"The Lord highlighted you to me. Did you hurt yourself?"

"Yes, I recently had knee surgery." He gave me a few more details.

"Can I pray for you?"

"Certainly!"

I put my hand on the back of his arm and we both closed our eyes. As I prayed, I felt a strong sense of the Lord's pleasure over him, as I often do, but I felt this man had weathered many trials and had continued to persevere in his faith. I expressed this in my prayer and then I saw a picture. "I'm seeing a picture of a field bursting forth with some sort of crop. It looks similar to wheat, but has larger heads. Things that you have believed, toiled and sown for are going to spring forth very soon." I continued in prayer, "Thank you, Father, for this godly man who has followed you faithfully. Bless him in every way. Amen."

We chatted for a few more minutes. "I have been a Christian for many years, and the picture you saw and the prayer you prayed really encouraged me," he said with a kind smile.

He mentioned that he worked for one of the ministries that I was familiar with at The Hope Center, so we talked about it for a few moments. I had to cut our visit a little short, explaining I was waiting for someone, and I quickly went back inside.

When I walked back in the building, neither of the ladies had come down to escort me to their office, so I struck up a conversation with the security guard, speaking prophetic words of encouragement and pointing out his godly character. I ended up praying for him to find a job, and that God would bless him and his family in every way. We continued to talk about Jesus until I saw a lady on the other side of the lobby heading toward me.

"I've been struggling with discouragement lately," he said. "This lifted my spirits. Thank you!"

"It was an honor to meet you! God has incredible things in store for you and your family. God bless you." I shook his hand and turned to go.

Thank you, Holy Spirit, for allowing me to express Your heart of love to these two men today. I know You will continue to build them up in Your love and tenderness. Everything about them is special to Your heart.

SATURDAY, MARCH 8th

❧Working Prayers❧

Work situations can present challenges for sharing God's love gifts, but they always allow tremendous opportunities to do battle in the heavenlies. After I set up my table display for my event staffing job at a grocery store, I immediately began praying.

Lord, I claim this store for You. Touch every person that works here and every person who comes through these doors today and every day. Permeate their hearts with Your love and open their eyes to Your truth....

As people came to my table to get a sample of a hot, buttered tortilla, I did my best to make their day a little cheerier. After presenting my spiel about the tortillas, I tried to engage them in friendly conversation. Most conversations were short because people were in a hurry to shop, but one woman in her 70's seemed lonely, so we chatted about various things for a while. Then the conversation turned serious.

"I've had a painful year," she said.

"I'm sorry. Why's that?" I figured if she brought it up then she may want to talk about it.

"My most significant relationship ended and I've battled serious health issues. My health is better now, but I've experienced a lot of loss."

"I'm so sorry. God wants you to know how much He loves you. You are important and special to Him. When we ask Jesus to forgive us, God's Spirit is able to live in us. Then He is able to give us strength and wisdom for every trial." She was very open and receptive, so I continued. "I've been a Christian since I was young, and God's been such a help through all of my painful times. I know He wants to wrap His arms around you and walk with you through life." We talked for a few more minutes until another customer walked up. "I'll be praying for you. God bless you!"

"Thank you. I'm sorry to take so much of your time."

"It was my pleasure. Good-bye and take care."

Jesus, show her Your love! I continued to pray for her and for others as they came to sample my extra thin, tasty tortillas, grateful God truly works through our prayers.

❧A Miss and Ice❧

After five-and-a-half hours on my feet standing in one spot, I was happy to get home and kick my feet up for a few minutes before Ron and I headed to a Bible study at Stuart and Nancy Gurnea's house.

On the way to the meeting, we stopped by Sprouts to pick up some organic produce. Since I was tired, I only shared friendly chatter with a few people. When we got to the checkout, a dark-haired young man began ringing up our items.

The thought popped into my head that he had been home schooled.

Rather than jump right in and ask, I took the easy route. "Are you in college?"

"Yes." We talked about where he was going and what he was studying.

"Where did you go to high school?" I asked. He named one of the nearby public schools. We chatted until he finished with our groceries. "Good-bye. God bless you," I said.

"Good-bye."

Well, unless he was home schooled during his elementary years, I totally missed that one. I should have been more bold and just asked him if he had been home schooled. That whole conversation seemed pretty lame, actually. I chuckled.

But on the positive side, Lord, at least I was able to show interest in his life and let him know in a small way that he is important. Touch him with Your love, Jesus, even though I didn't do a very impressive job. I chuckled again as we unloaded the groceries into the back of the van.

We left Sprouts and drove to the Gurnea's house. They had invited an Australian friend and evangelist, Jeffrey Fazl, to speak and minister this weekend while he was in the U.S. This was the second meeting I had attended. Jeffrey shared the importance of his love relationship with Jesus, and he told the story of his church transforming from a place of seeing very few healings, to 80% of his church being healed and over 95% healed when he travels to Indonesia. He talked about the importance of breaking off the demonic lies that hinder us from receiving the healing that has already been paid for by Jesus.

As he spoke, I prayed silently: *Stop the demonic lies telling me and Ron that we can't be healed. I will listen to those lies no longer! Free us from them, Holy Spirit, so that Your truth is all we hear in every area of our lives.*

After the teaching, people were encouraged to ask for prayer or find others who needed prayer. The Holy Spirit impressed upon me a woman across the room that I had never met, so I introduced myself and asked if I could pray for her. As I began to pray, I saw a picture in my mind's eye of a huge field covered in thick ice that was trying to crush the life out of the grass in the field. I explained the picture to her as I prayed.

"You are the field of grass and Satan has sent numerous trials in your life in an attempt to crush and destroy you. But because you have allowed God's love and warmth to flow through you no matter how difficult the trials have been, the warmth of God's love flowing through you—the grass—has been melting the ice from underneath, which in turn has watered the grass and produced beautiful flowers. I am now seeing flowers of all types and colors bursting forth and breaking apart the ice. All the trials Satan sent your way to destroy you have been watering the flowers of your heart and making you resplendently beautiful and powerful in the Lord."

What a sweet picture, Father, of the power of Your love in our lives in the midst of trials.

SUNDAY, MARCH 9th

We had another evening gathering, and after the meeting I was asked to join several others in praying for a sweet husband and wife who were new to the group. Stuart did the majority of the praying, but as he prayed I saw a picture of a huge wrought-iron fence. I saw the gates swing open and the couple hold hands and skip out into the sunrise. They were playing and laughing, and having tremendous fun with one another.

I shared this picture with them and then said, "The Holy Spirit is freeing you from the demonic attack that has been wearing you down." The wife nodded in agreement as I spoke. "Your main assignment right now is to delight in each other and delight in the Lord. He will bring the freedom, victory and powerful ministry you long for as you simply enjoy Him and each other."

MARCH 10th—14th

I have been extremely busy so the interactions I had Monday through Friday weren't written down. Oops! Most of my time was spent working on things for CAYM or typing this book, so I don't think I left the house much.

❧Working with the Comforter❧

When I walked into the sanctuary of a friend's church, my eyes immediately went to a white-haired gentleman sitting in a wheelchair on the back row.

"He's discouraged," the thought came suddenly. I knew it was the Holy Spirit, so I immediately headed toward the man and the younger gentleman sitting beside him.

"Hi! My name's Julie."

The younger gentleman made the introductions. "My name is Matt and this is my father, Allen." We shook hands.

"As soon as I walked in here a few moments ago," I said to Allen, "I sensed God's love for you and that He wants to encourage you. You have been discouraged and even feeling hopeless, and the Lord wants to wrap you in His love and free you from the lies and attacks of the enemy. You are special beyond comparison to God's heart and He wants you to know He is here to comfort and heal you."

A smile spread across his face and his eyes glistened with tears. "Thank you."

We talked for several minutes and I shared a few more impressions from the Holy Spirit. Allen expressed his gratitude again, and then it was time to sit down, so I sat in the back row with them, just one seat away from Matt.

Matt leaned over and spoke, "Thank you for sharing that with my father. He has been extremely discouraged and unhappy. He's been in a nursing home and is depressed, especially since his hip surgery." As we continued to talk, I found out his father hadn't been in church for three months. *Thanks, Holy Spirit, for bringing him to church today so that You could encourage his heart.*

After the service, I asked if I could pray for Allen. He was happy to have me pray, so I sat beside him and placed my hand on his shoulder.

"Lord, how You love Allen. He delights Your heart. Allow him to feel Your arms of love around him. Break off all the lies and attacks of the enemy and free him from depression and discouragement in Jesus' name. We take authority against all lying spirits and command them to be silent. Holy Spirit, Spirit of Truth, pour out the truth of Your love into Allen's heart all day long every day. You have many plans and purposes for Allen. You are freeing his tongue and breaking off fear of man so that he can boldly share Your love in that nursing home. Many people will be encouraged and brought to Your love through Allen. Make him as bold as a lion and as gentle as a dove...."

I prayed for several minutes, and I felt faith and hope rising in his spirit. When I finished praying, his eyes were glistening with not only tears, but with renewed hope. We talked a little longer and I hugged his neck again.

His son, Matt, was standing nearby so I asked the Holy Spirit if there was anything for him. I had the thought that there were changes happening in his job situation.

"Are you looking for another job or trying to start your own business?" I asked.

He looked a little surprised. "Yes, I've been teaching high school, but have been applying to teach at the college level." We continued to talk about what he had been hoping for, and then I prayed for him. The Holy Spirit encouraged Matt's heart and re-minded him through this simple word that He knows and cares about every detail in his life.

MONDAY, MARCH 17th

❧Joseph and an Egg Encounter❧

Sierra came by, so after helping her with her banking and praying with her for wisdom to make good choices, I followed her to the title transfer office to get her car title changed from Ron's name to hers. I didn't feel any impressions to say anything to the lady who was helping us.

Lord, bless her and fill her with Your love.

After saying good-bye to Sierra, I drove to the grocery store to grab a few items. I saw my friend, Joseph, the produce manager, working hard as usual organizing the produce.

"How are you today?" I asked.

"Not very good. I have some sort of painful sinus infection," he said. We talked about it for a few moments and then I placed my hand on the back of his arm and prayed with my eyes opened.

"Lord, bring your healing in Jesus' name. I break off this illness and pray the infection will be gone in Jesus' mighty name. Bless Joseph physically, emotionally and spiritually. How you love Him! Amen."

Joseph is used to me talking about the Lord's dealings in my life, and I've prayed for him before, so I'm sure he wasn't surprised. I'm hoping sometime soon to take him and his wife out for a meal and explain in depth God's love for them, and to share my story of how God's love has transformed my life. I didn't befriend him to preach to him, but since he has become my friend, I want him and his wife to know how amazing it is to walk with God.

I didn't feel any impressions to share more than friendly comments until I was at the back of the store. There was a lady, probably in her early seventies, standing near the eggs with a boot cast on her right foot and a crutch under her right arm. She looked uncomfortable.

"That must have hurt," I said, pointing to her foot.

"Yes, it did!" She told me how she injured her foot.

"Can I pray for you?" I put my hand on her arm.

"Yes," she said as she bowed her head. I bowed my head with her and prayed for healing and blessing, and spoke of God's incredible love for her.

She interrupted me, "Please pray for my son, too. He had a stroke six years ago and can barely function or talk. I'm his caregiver."

"Lord, bring physical, emotional and spiritual blessings and healing to her son…."

When I finished praying, we spoke for over twenty minutes about her son's situation, the Lord's grace in their lives and finding a church to keep her spiritually encouraged. This precious woman is selflessly laying down her life for her grown son, and it was an honor to encourage her for her faithfulness and love, and believe with her for healing.

TUESDAY, MARCH 18ᵗʰ

I made a quick trip to Sam's Club. I didn't have any interactions because I was in a hurry to buy food for our new neighbors whose twenty-year-old son was tragically killed in a car wreck while on his way to visit them from California several weeks ago. They had immediately left for California, and had just returned a few days ago.

I zipped home and cooked the meal while praying again for this dear, heartbroken family. They weren't home at suppertime, like the teenage daughter thought they would be, so I decided to try again in the morning to deliver the food.

WEDNESDAY, MARCH 19ᵗʰ

❧*Prayers for Grace*❧

I walked across the street and delivered the meal I had made for the neighbors, along with some flowers and a card. The father was home and we spoke briefly outside in the driveway.

"I can't even imagine your pain," I said as tears welled up in my eyes. He told me the family wasn't doing well. It still seemed unreal to him, and his wife was crying all the time. "Can I pray for you right now?" I asked.

"Yes," he said. I put my hand on his arm and we both bowed our heads and closed our eyes.

"Oh, Father, how You love this family. Please allow them to feel Your arms of love around them during this awful time. Help them receive Your comfort and strength for the days ahead. Fill them with Your peace and grace, and mend their broken hearts. Protect them from the lies and attacks of Satan that will try to turn their grief to anger and tear their family apart. I pray they will grow closer together as a family as they learn to better love each other in the midst of their overwhelming pain. Heal and restore each dear member of this family. Amen." We both wiped away tears when I finished praying.

Comforter, come and heal their hearts as only You can.

Chapter 8

Still Marching

❧Divine Leading❧

I had two options.

Option one: Drive fifteen minutes west to buy organic produce from Sprouts. Option two: Drive seven minutes east and play with my grandson, Ryder.

I headed east.

Richelle and I visited as I chased and tickled Ryder; built towers with Mega Blocks that he kindly knocked down; and cuddled with him whenever I could squeeze in a few seconds of hugs.

I stayed for about an hour and then pulled myself away to finish my other errands. I knew I could buy reasonably priced organic apples from WinCo, which was just minutes from Richelle's house, but instead of going to Winco, I headed to the library first. I almost turned around because I'm frugal and don't like to waste time or extra pennies on mileage, but for some reason I continued driving to the library.

After I found the books I needed on nonprofit corporations, I carried the stack downstairs, passing a young lady dressed all in black wearing a spiked choker necklace. She was sitting in a chair texting on her phone. The Holy Spirit highlighted her to me, so I turned back around and walked up to her.

"Hi! When I walked past you, I felt a strong impression of God's love for you. You are special to Him. He has given you the ability to see things in a way that the rest of us can't see. He wants you to know it is a gift and He is going to keep developing that gift."

She smiled and nodded her head, "That's very true. I do." We talked a little longer about that gift.

"I can tell your heart is soft and open, and I'm seeing a picture in my mind's eye of you opening a window as the sun is rising. There is darkness behind you representing your past," she nodded her head in affirmation. "But I see you jumping through that window into God's light. I see you dancing and laughing in God's presence. Do you have a relationship with the Lord?"

"I was saved and baptized when I was younger."

"That's wonderful. God is going to continue to deepen your love relationship with Him as you spend time in His presence. He is speaking to your thoughts, so listen to Him, talk with Him and read the wonderful truths He's given in the Bible. You are going to see amazing changes in your life, and you will be dancing in His light and love."

She shared more of her story as I asked a few questions. She told me she was about to move out and share rent with a guy who was a friend.

"Living with a guy can create all kinds of temptations, even if you're just friends now," I said. "The Lord also wants us to avoid even the appearance of evil, so I would lovingly encourage you not to move in with him. The Lord will make other ways for you to live on your own if you ask Him for guidance." We continued to talk for several minutes until her mother arrived to pick her up.

"God bless you," I said. "Never forget how special and loved you are."

"Thank you," she said with a beautiful smile. "Good-bye."

I checked out my books, making friendly conversation with the librarian, and then got back in the van. I decided to go to WinCo next since I had once again talked myself out of driving all the way to Sprouts. All I needed were the apples, dried dates and gluten-free crackers.

I arrived at Winco, picked out the apples and then walked over to the bulk section. I turned into the aisle where the dates were located, and was shocked to see someone I hadn't seen in eleven years, but for whom I had been praying all that time. Last I knew, this person lived more than an hour away. This story is too personal to share, but I have no doubt the Holy Spirit directed me to that exact aisle at that exact moment. All my changes of plans, and even the conversation at the library, were all part of bringing me to this extremely significant meeting. I was again in awe of God's brilliance, and grateful for His ability to lead my steps.

❧Victorious Victor❧

When I finished with that significant conversation, I found the crackers and got in line to check out. I rarely notice the names of cashiers who ring up my items, but my eyes fell on Victor's name-tag. He gave me a friendly greeting as he began ringing up my items.

"Hello, Victor! I believe your name is very significant. God has called you to victory." I don't usually jump in so quickly, but he smiled and looked pleasantly surprised, so I continued. "God loves you so very much. In my mind's eye I'm seeing a great battle with warring going on in the heavenlies over you, and the angels have won. I see chains coming off your ankles and wrists, and areas where you have struggled, you are being set free."

"Wow! That's cool," he said.

"I'm reminded of the verse that says, *'Let us throw off everything that hinders and the sin that so easily entangles, and let us run with perseverance the race marked out for us'* (Hebrews 12:1). The Lord is breaking off those areas that have held you back and discouraged you." He continued to nod and smile. "Are you a believer?" I asked, though I was pretty sure he was.

"Yes! I play keyboards at church." I asked what church he attended and we talked about that for a moment.

I wasn't getting any of this information ahead of time. I just opened my mouth and started speaking, praying the Holy Spirit was guiding my words. "I see a powerful anointing on you for worship and song writing. I also see you working with youth."

"Man. All of that is right. I do work with the youth group at church."

"Never doubt the calling and the anointing on your life. As you continue to draw nearer and nearer to Jesus, that anointing and power will increase."

Victor was excited and encouraged—and so was I. The Holy Spirit was increasing my ability to hear details just like He told me He would after I stood up in the theatre. These details, like the details at the library earlier, only came because I stepped out on the water by faith and began speaking.

Thank You, Holy Spirit. You love to bless people with Your gifts. It's an honor to work with You on Your GPS route. I love You! Keep increasing what You're doing.

THURSDAY, MARCH 20th

❧Drips from Heaven❧

I had picked up my sweet friend, Margi, from the airport last night, and we were enjoying a wonderful visit. She and her daughter, Johanna, my adopted niece, moved to Colorado two-and-a-half years ago, and Margi had come back for a reunion and to visit with friends in the area for five days. I dropped her off at her friend's house this morning, and then swung by a grocery store to look for my favorite barbeque sauce (Garland Jack's) for the brisket I was making on Sunday for a CAYM vision and brainstorm meeting.

As I was looking for the sauce, I started to feel guilty because I didn't have any *umph* to say anything to anyone at the store, but I honestly wasn't feeling like the Holy Spirit was highlighting anyone. I realized the enemy was trying to make me feel guilty again, so I rebuked his lies and reminded myself that God wants me to enjoy life—not walk around in guilt.

After I bought the barbeque sauce, I talked briefly with a young man raising money outside the store. I donated a few dollars to the cause, but I didn't have any promptings for him either. After a short, friendly interchange, I said, "God bless you," and left.

I was going to try again to go to Sprouts, but my van was in desperate need of washing, so I made a last-minute decision to clean the van first, taking the necessary exit off the highway.

When I arrived at the car wash, I saw a middle-aged woman using a sprayer hose to spray the ground, so I figured she was the manager or owner. I had a question, so I walked toward where she was working.

"Hello! How are you? Are you the owner or manager?" I asked.

"I'm both," she said with a friendly tone and smile.

She answered my question and I walked back to my car. She came over a moment later to tell me they were having problems with some of the sprayers, so to let her know if I had any problems with mine.

"You look really familiar," I said. "Do you go to church here in McKinney?"

"No. I go to Kingdom Hall [a Jehovah Witness church] in Frisco."

We tried to figure out how else we might know each other since she said I looked familiar, too, but we couldn't figure it out. She went back to what she was doing and I started the sprayer to wash the van.

Lord, do you have anything for her? I continued to pray as I washed the van. When I switched from rinse to foam brush, the soap began leaking out of the fittings in the ceiling and dripping a little on my head. I tried to dodge the drips, grateful I didn't have big plans for the evening. I called her over so she could see what was happening.

She apologized as she watched me do my drip-dodging dance. "It's no big deal. I don't have important plans this evening," I laughed.

When I finished, she wanted to give me a free spot-free rinse, so she asked me to move the van forward to get it out of the way of the dripping soap. I got in the van and drove it forward while she rinsed it. I continued to pray for her, and when she finished, I rolled down my window to thank her. We talked a few more minutes about the car wash, and then I felt that *umph* I hadn't felt earlier in the day. "I used to live across from people who were Jehovah Witnesses, so I studied and compared the Jehovah Witness' teachings with the Bible," I said.

"What did you find out?" she asked.

We proceeded to have a long, friendly conversation as I shared the discrepancies with their teachings and the Bible, and as she shared her viewpoint.

"One part that makes me sad," I said, "is all the laws and rules that Jehovah Witnesses and other religions have set up for their people. Jesus came to free us from laws. When we ask Him to forgive us and live inside us, it's His love that makes us want to do what's right. We no longer have to be given a set of guidelines by an organization. The more time we spend with the Lord, the more we fall in love with Him and can't help but honor Him in all we do."

I presented everything in love, not attacking her personally, but gently presenting my concerns with the teachings and false prophecies of the Jehovah Witness church. She had been a Baptist when she was younger, but from some comments she made, I don't think she began studying the Bible until the Jehovah Witnesses began sharing with her verses taken out of context to make their point. I kindly shared with her the importance of really knowing the Bible for ourselves so that we can recognize when teachings are taken out of context and don't line up with the whole Bible.

We talked for thirty or forty minutes before I realized I had better get going and let her get going. She had given me her phone number earlier so that I could let her know if the spot-free rinse worked or not, so I told her I would get back with her.

Holy Spirit, keep working in her heart. I break off the religious lies of the enemy that are keeping her from Your truth. You said we must believe on the Lord Jesus Christ to be saved, but she believes in a false Jesus and a false set of rules in which she's trying to earn her way to her version of heaven. In all her efforts, she still doesn't know You.

I am reminded of what You said, Jesus, in Matthew 7:23 about what would happen on judgment day. Many will list all the good things, even amazing things, they did for God on the earth, but Jesus "will tell them plainly, 'I never knew you. Away from me, you evildoers!'"

Open her eyes, Holy Spirit. Help her to come to know who You truly are.

In hindsight, I'm glad I didn't stop to talk with people at the grocery store when I wasn't feeling any promptings. If I had, I would have missed the perfect timing of the drips from heaven to bring this dear woman and me together.

SATURDAY, MARCH 22ⁿᵈ

❧God's Rapper❧

I drove Margi to the nearby Enterprise car rental location so that she could rent a vehicle for the weekend. This particular Enterprise is located in a strip mall next door to a driver's education school. I pulled into an open space in front of the driving school and there were seven guys—black, white and Hispanic—who all looked to be in their twenties, waiting outside in front of the school. Several were smoking and they all looked intimidating.

"I'm nervous to get out," Margi chuckled.

Her comment made me chuckle, too, but it was noon and there were plenty of people around. "I'll wait here for a few minutes to make sure you don't have any problems renting the car," I said.

She got out and I began praying for the young men on the sidewalk in front of me. *Lord, I'm here and these young men are here. Show me if You have anything for them. Have You brought us together for a reason?*

I began feeling like I was supposed to talk with them, but my nerves kicked in and doubts came. *There are a lot of them, and I'm not especially presentable in my sweats and T-shirt with no make-up and un-fixed hair. But, again, it's not about me.*

I feel your prompting, Holy Spirit, but can You please give me some-thing ahead of time to boost my confidence a little? What popped into my thoughts was that one of the men was gifted musically. *Okay. I'll go for it.*

Margi had waved me on a few moments earlier, so I knew she was fine. I got out of the van and stepped up onto the sidewalk, just to the left of the group. They all looked at me quizzically.

"Hi," I said. "I just dropped my friend off to get a rental car and I was praying God's blessings over you all. As I prayed, I felt there was someone here who was gifted musically."

"I am," said the black gentleman closest to me. "Are you a psy-chic?" he asked as he continued to smoke his cigarette.

"No. When you ask Jesus to forgive you, God's Spirit is able to live inside you. He speaks to me all the time for my own benefit, and I've been asking Him to speak to me for other people." I kept talking, praying it was the Holy Spirit directing my words. "You had a relationship with Christ when you were little, and your parents have been praying for you."

"Yeah, that's right. Are you sure you're not a psychic?" he laughed.

I chuckled with him. "No, I'm just trying to hear what the Lord is telling me. God has given you a tremendous anointing in music and the enemy knows how powerful it is. The demons have been working hard to keep you away from a relationship with God because it is from that love relationship that the anointing will flow." By this time the rest of the young men had turned back to their other conversations, but this young man, whom I'll call Archie, asked me to step away from the group so he could hear me better. "I see God freeing you from the lies of the enemy and drawing you into a love relationship that you never dreamed possible."

"I'm not in bondage," he said with confusion on his face.

"Well, what these chains represent are lies that keep us from running our race and living the life God has for us—a life of walking in His love and wisdom, and doing what He's called us to do. I am seeing you receiving songs—lyrics and tunes—directly from heaven, and many people being impacted by those songs."

"I'm a rapper and I already impact people with my music." He wasn't at all defensive, but was merely stating the facts.

"Yes, you do impact people, but this impact from heaven will bring people into a relationship with Jesus and their lives will be changed. Does what I'm saying make sense?"

"Yes, and I'm definitely listening because I've never had anyone approach me out of the blue like this before," he laughed and then snuffed out the cigarette he had finished.

"Yes, God is moving and doing new things in your heart and life."

We talked about the church he sometimes attends, and I encouraged him to surround himself with other Christians who are running hard after God. "Our friends will either drag us down and distract us, or encourage us in the things of God. I'll be praying you are able to connect with people and develop good friendships with other strong Christians who will encourage you spiritually."

"Yeah, I need that."

"Can I pray for you right now if I keep my eyes opened?"

"Sure," he said. "I don't mind at all."

I thought he meant he didn't care about me closing my eyes, so I put my hand on his shoulder and closed my eyes and prayed. A few sentences into the prayer, I looked up and saw his eyes were open, so I went ahead and kept mine open to make it more comfortable for him. "Lord, come and fill Archie with Your presence and allow him to feel Your love like he's never known before. Pour out Your power and strength. Surround him with other Christians who love You. Give him a growing hunger for more of You and Your presence. You have amazing things for this man of God...."

After we finished praying, he gave me his phone number and I told him there were a lot of amazing Christian rappers that he would enjoy listening to. He wasn't familiar with any, so I promised to text him information. We had been talking for over twenty minutes, and just two minutes after we finished praying, their break was over and the group of guys headed back into the driving school. God's timing is perfect.

Wow, Lord, this is the third person I've talked with this month whom You've called and anointed to lead people into Your presence through music and worship. Raise up worshipers all across the planet who will draw people to Your heart.

MONDAY, MARCH 24th

☙ Words for Children, a Veteran and Discounted Apples ☙

I journal what Jesus is saying to me three or four days per week. I sit at the computer and type up what He speaks to my thoughts. It often begins with, "Julie, I love you...." or "Good morning, beloved daughter...." Today, instead of listening for His words for me, I felt prompted to listen for His words for some friends of ours who left their home to share Jesus in another country. He gave me very specific prophetic words for each of their four young children, even for their daughter who was born just this week. Being this specific was another step of faith, but I emailed the words to them this morning. [I heard back from the parents later and they said the prophetic words made them feel loved and seemed liked they were accurate, but we won't know for sure until the kids grow up.]

⸎

A few hours later, I followed Margi to Enterprise to drop off her rental car. (No, there weren't any young men standing outside this time.) We drove to the grocery, and then to pay my car registration. Margi was on the phone with her daughter, so I ran in by myself to pay my registration fee. There was an older gentleman wearing a Vietnam Veteran's hat sitting on a bench just inside the door. The past few years I've tried harder to acknowledge and honor all military personnel, so I stopped for a moment and spoke with him.

"Thank you for all you've done for our country and the sacrifices you made for our freedom."

He acted surprised. "Thank you. I appreciate that," he said with a smile.

"I like to pray for people I'm around. Do you have any prayer needs?"

"No, I can't think of any, but thank you."

"Okay. God bless you and have a nice day."

"Thank you. You, too."

I continued on around the corner to the tax assessor collector's office, and was able to walk right up to the next available person.

"I'm surprised you aren't really busy with it being the end of the month," I said.

The gal looked puzzled and said, "It isn't the end of the month."

I paused a moment and then laughed. "You're right." I woke up thinking this was the last day to register, but I have another week. We continued to talk about our bad memories and the funny things we say as we age. Nothing came to mind to share with her from the Lord, so I prayed blessings for her, and was glad my silly slip-up added entertainment to her day.

⸎

Later that afternoon, I drove Margi back to the airport and we were able to talk about some important issues heavy on her heart.

138

After I dropped her off, I swung by Sprouts on the way home. I had been putting it off for five days. I was now tired and didn't have an ounce of desire to talk with anyone, but I submitted my heart to the Lord. *You know how I'm feeling, so change my heart if there is someone I need to talk with. I trust You even when I'm tired.*

I quickly made my way to the organic section and began getting fruits and vegetables. The Gala apples weren't marked, so I looked around for help with the price. The man I found ended up being the very friendly store manager. He went to find out the price, and when he came back, he told me he'd give me the same price as the cheaper red delicious apples beside them.

"That's sweet! How will you do that?" I asked

"I'll find you at the checkout and tell the cashier."

"Well, thank you. My husband eats several apples a day so we go through a lot every week." We talked for a few minutes about healthy eating before he headed back to what he was doing.

When I finished with my shopping, he found me at the checkout and helped me unload my groceries and we continued to chat. I asked questions about his job and family, and he said they were buying a house that wasn't far from a church we had attended several years before.

I mentioned the church to him. "Have you ever visited there?"

"No, we haven't, but we have friends who go there." I recognized their names, but didn't know them personally.

"I hope you visit! It's a good church. You'll enjoy it."

"We might just do that."

As I pushed my cart out to the van, I mused over my discounted apples and the seemingly small encounter. *Lord, that seemed like a really insignificant encounter, but are any encounters really insignificant? Maybe our chat will stick in his memory, and he and his family will begin going to church and draw near to Your heart. Bless them in every way. How You love them.*

I drove home, put away the groceries, ate supper and popped the new movie *Frozen* into the DVD player, laughing at the well-written humor while visiting with Dane. *Thanks, Lord, for laughter and a little time to chill out.*

WEDNESDAY, MARCH 26th

❧How's Your Heart?❧

I used to shop once a week for groceries, but since we are trying to eat gluten-free and organic, I have to shop at four different stores throughout the week. On the bright side, at least it's good for more opportunities to talk with people. I made my grocery run today, but didn't have anything more than a few friendly chats until I was ready to check out. My cashier was a lovely young woman, who I later learned was a senior in high school.

"Hello, how are you?" I asked.

"I'm well. How are you?"

It was the customary polite greeting, but her eyes looked sad. *Jesus, please bless this dear gal.* "How's your heart?" the question popped out of my mouth.

"Excuse me?" she asked.

"I was praying God would bless you because I sensed your heart was hurting." Her eyes grew wide with surprise and I continued. "It's because of a relationship," I said. She nodded and I could tell her eyes were getting emotional. I knew this wasn't the place for her to cry, so I lightened things up. "Guy issues can be tough, but God has a good man for you."

I continued to pray for her as I put more bags of groceries in my cart. When she was almost finished checking my groceries, I gently said, "I see a picture of you as a beautiful flower and you have been painfully crushed, but God is healing your heart and you will spring back even more beautiful than ever." She smiled, but still couldn't say anything. "God bless you. I'll be praying for you."

"Good-bye," she said with a faint smile.

Jesus, heal her heart. She is Your precious flower.

THURSDAY, MARCH 27th

❧Gifts of Love on the Phone❧

The Lord prompted me to deliver a few gifts of love and concern over the phone. I began by sending several texts.

TO ARCHIE: Hi Archie! This is Julie. We met and spoke in front of the driving school on Saturday. How are you? God has powerful things for you on this earth! It was no accident we met. I'm confident God set up our meeting. I Googled Christian rappers for you and found a long list. Lecrae seems to be a favorite and is having a huge impact with his words. (I then told Archie how to find him on YouTube.) Once you watch some of his videos, I'd love to hear your thoughts. Have a great day. You are a world changer and will draw many hearts to the God who loves them and wants to forgive them and give them incredible purpose for their lives! Blessings! ☺

TO ME: Thanks, Julie ☺

[We then talked about my being busy writing this book, and him busy writing music. It was a positive, but short conversation.]

TO THE LADY FROM THE CAR WASH: Hi! This is Julie. We met at your car wash and spoke for quite a while. ☺ How are you? I did want to tell you the spot-free side did have less spots. It wasn't spot-free, but definitely better. ☺ I enjoyed talking with you and had several thoughts since we spoke. Do you have an email you would want to share or are you on Facebook? Blessings and thanks again for all your friendly help.

TO ME: [No response. I'll keep praying for her and maybe send a text with a few of those thoughts. The worse she would do is erase the messages before she reads them.]

PHONE MESSAGE LEFT FOR ALLEN: Hi, Allen. This is Julie. I met you at church and prayed with you. I was checking in to see how you are doing. I still feel the Lord's amazing love for you and I pray you are feeling His loving arms around you during your hard situation. I'm confident God's going to use you to bless a lot of people in the nursing home as His love flows through you. Be encouraged and don't forget how important you are to the Father. God bless you!

[I didn't expect a response because of his age. I'll try to call again soon.]

BUSINESS PHONE CALL: I called and discussed life insurance questions with Andrew, the friendly agent who answered the phone, but before we hung up I asked him, "Do you have any prayer needs? I pray blessings on people I interact with."

"That's awesome," he said enthusiastically. "In all my years, I've never had anyone ask me that. I need prayer to slow down throughout my work day and spend some time alone in the Lord's presence, reading the Bible and talking with Him. Work is constantly busy and I need to make God a higher priority in my day." We talked about the importance of making time for the Lord and a little about Andrew's spiritual background.

"Do you mind if I just pray for you right now?" I asked.

"That'd be great!"

"Lord, thank You for Your love for Andrew. Bless him and his family in every way....Help him make more time to seek Your presence since that is the desire of his heart. Bring a new boldness into his spirit and break off all fear of man, fear of failure and fear of rejection. Increase his faith to hear You and give him words of knowledge, insight and revelation for those he is around. You love Him and have fun things in store for him! Amen!"

"Thank you again. That really made my week!"

FRIDAY, MARCH 28th

I made several business phone calls today, but didn't feel any promptings to say anything other than, "God bless you," at the end of the conversations.

Ron and I went out to eat this evening, but I didn't share anything special with the waiter. When he told us his allergies were messing with his voice, I said I'd be praying for him.

SUNDAY, MARCH 30th

❧*God's Not Dead!*❧

Well, Lord, I'm back in a theatre. I hope You don't ask me to stand up again. No...forget I said that. I trust You. I'll do whatever You prompt my heart to do.

I was at the early-bird discount showing of the movie *God's Not*

Dead. It was only playing in expensive theatres, so the discount was helpful. My parents had decided to join me, which was a nice treat. Because it was 10 a.m. there were only about twenty of us in the showing, but I had heard the movie was doing very well and had been number four in box office sales on its opening weekend.

Proving God is real is a huge topic, but the screenwriters did a great job incorporating a number of important points that people don't understand such as evolution's circular reasoning and the existence of evil due to Satan's influence on the earth and our free will to choose right or wrong. My only regret was that I hadn't brought any tissues with me because they wove several emotional and true-to-life stories into the movie, showing how God loves us and helps us deal with pain, abandonment and death.

When the movie was over and the credits began running, I immediately wondered if the two men sitting in the row in front of us were believers, so I decided to find out. I ignored the small trace of fear and headed their way.

They were still sitting, so I crouched down behind them and asked in a friendly, excited tone, "Are you guys believers?"

"Yeah," the older of the two said, rather startled.

"I'm glad! Wasn't that a great movie?"

"Yes, it was," he said as they stood up to leave. They looked like a father and son.

"Do you go to church around here?" I asked.

They told me where they went.

"I've heard good things about that church." We talked for a few more moments as we headed toward the aisle. "God bless you."

"Thanks. You too," the father said with a friendly smile.

My parents were headed to the exit near the front of the theatre, but I stopped to pray for a moment since no one was behind me.

Lord, do you want me to say anything to anyone else since a number of people are still sitting here?

I felt a *yes* in my spirit, so I walked forward and turned into the next closest aisle where a lady and her daughter were sitting. As I got closer I sensed they were Christians.

"You guys are believers, aren't you?"

"Yes," the mother said with a sweet smile on her face.

"Wasn't that a great movie?" We chatted for a few moments about the quality of Christian movies coming out lately.

When we finished talking, I continued to walk toward the exit, passing another older couple still sitting and talking to each other. I stepped into their aisle and had a similar conversation with them and the lady in front of them.

It was fun talking with other believers, and I felt sort of like an usher walking people toward the door as we talked about the movie and Jesus.

When I finally arrived at the exit, two young ladies were standing on each side of a large trash can, talking and waiting to begin cleaning.

"Hi! Have you two seen this movie yet?" I asked them.

"No," they both responded.

"Oh, you've got to see it! It's really well done and is helpful for people who are wondering if God is real."

"I was planning on seeing it," one of the gals said.

"Me, too," said the other.

"Are you Christians?" I asked.

"Well, not really. I've visited different churches in the past," said one of the gals.

"I'm Catholic, but not practicing," the other said.

With a loving tone and a big smile, I briefly shared what came to mind of my story. "I asked Jesus to forgive me and live inside me when I was seven years old, and having a relationship with Him has made all the difference in the world. The Lord has helped me with marriage, parenting and all the challenges I've had in my life. I have such love for Him that I often feel a bubbling in my spirit—a bubbling joy—because of His love and care for me."

They were listening with interest, so I continued. "We were created to walk with God through life so that He can love us and we can love Him. He loves the two of you so very much. I can feel His love as we're standing here."

"Aw, that's so sweet," one of them said. Both the girls were open and very interested in what I was saying.

"Jesus wants to forgive both of you so that He can live inside you and guide you through life. I feel like you are both very close to beginning a relationship with God. I realize you need to get back to work, so let me give you my number in case you want to call to talk or pray." I wrote down my number and we talked a few more moments.

"I know you need to get to work, but can I pray really fast for both of you?

"Sure," they said with enthusiasm in their voices.

We huddled around the trash can and I put one hand on each of their shoulders.

"Lord, how You love these two! This was no accident that we met here. You are drawing their hearts to Your love. Bless them in every way and fill them with Your love. Allow them to hear You and come to know You as their Savior and Friend. You have incredible things in store for both of them. Amen!"

"Thank you," they both said with obvious appreciation.

"Let me give you guys hugs," I said, and then gave them both a quick hug. "You are very special to God! I'm excited for all He is going to do in your lives. I had better let you get to work. God bless you both!"

"Thank you again! Bye!" They headed into the theatre and I finally headed out. My parents were kindly waiting for me.

Wow, that was fun! And You didn't ask me to stand up and shout to everyone this time. It's not about formulas or always doing the same things. It's about listening and responding. I love walking with You.

⸻

My parents and I stopped by Costco after the movie, and I shopped quickly in order to honor their time and because we were all hungry and ready for lunch. I exchanged a few friendly words here and there with people, praying silently for several people as we passed, but my main focus was on speed. The Holy Spirit knows we have schedules and the people we're with have schedules, and He takes all that into consideration when He works with us on our GPS routes.

MONDAY, MARCH 31ˢᵗ

❧Sweet Hannah❧

After working on this book all day, I was happy to take the trash out and enjoy the lovely spring weather after supper. The nine-year-old neighbor girl from down the street was riding her bike nearby, so I called a greeting to her.

"Hi, Hannah! How are you?"

"I'm good. How are you?"

"Doing great and loving this weather!" I walked toward the mailbox and she rode up to me. "How is school going for you?"

"It's okay. We have the STAAR test tomorrow." We talked about the test and a few other topics for about five minutes.

"Is there anything you need prayer for when I think of you?" It's the first time I'd been prompted to ask her this.

"Yes, my grandma has two friends that are sick." We talked about their illnesses and I told her I'd be praying. "I go to classes every week at our Catholic church and they are praying, too."

I shared with Hannah a little bit of my story and how I came to know Jesus. "I learned that Jesus came so we could have a relationship with Him rather than live under a list of laws and rules. Once Jesus is living inside us, we can't help but love others and do the right thing because we love Jesus so much."

We talked a little longer and then I asked, "Do you have a Bible you are able to read?"

"No, the dog got a hold of mine and chewed it up."

"I think I have a few extra Bibles. Would you want to read the Bible if I gave you one?"

"Yes. I'd read it. I liked it when I read some of the Bible before."

"I'll look for it and get it to you in the next couple days if that's okay."

"Thanks!"

We finished up the conversation and she headed down the road on her bike.

Holy Spirit, bless Hannah. She has such a tender spirit. Maybe she and I can read the Bible together once or twice a week if it's all right with her parents. Guide me in the time You want me to invest in this sweet young lady. If it's Your will, then You'll provide the time. I know nine year olds are very important to Your heart, so if You don't use me, use others to help Hannah grow in Your love for her!

Chapter 9

Other Radicals I Know

I filled this book with my personal stories to encourage you that one ordinary person can make a difference by simply following God's promptings. But to shake things up a bit and to prove that anyone can live this lifestyle, I asked a few friends and family members to each share one of their stories of saying *yes* to God's promptings.

BARBARA SHIPPY

Barbara is part of my writers' group and was a tremendous blessing and encouragement to me as I wrote this book. She leads incredible Bible studies and exercise classes at her church, and is a treasure. Here is her story:

❧*Cussed Out in Church*❧

It was Saturday evening when my husband Mike and I arrived at church. Carmen, a Christian songwriter and singer, was presenting a concert titled "There Is No Plan B", and we knew the church would be packed.

Since Mike was serving on the concert security team, we arrived before the doors officially opened. Because of my failing eyesight, Myron, our church's minister of music, allowed me to find a seat up close before anyone else entered the sanctuary. As I sat down, I placed items on the pew to save three extra seats, two to my right and one to my left. Within a few minutes of the doors opening, a family of four moved into the pew and sat to my right. A young man in his twenties who was apparently part of this family sat directly next to me, moving the items I had used to save the two seats. As he sat down, I welcomed him and told him I had been saving these places, politely asking him to move down the pew.

Looking directly at me and speaking in an insolent tone he said, "So?"

A little surprised by his response, I told him the spaces I had been saving were for two friends who would be late in arriving because their babysitter for their ninety-nine-year-old mother was late. I again asked him to please move down the pew.

Looking directly at me again, he replied, "So what. I don't care. They should have arrived before we did."

At this point, I was becoming pretty frustrated over the situation. For the third time, I politely asked him to move further to the right since there was plenty of room for him and his family.

In a much louder voice that could be heard several pews away, he emphatically stated, "I am not moving. Your friends can find another seat." His family immediately stood up, at the urging of his mother, to move to another pew. Just as he was exiting our row, he turned to me and said several awful, vulgar things very loudly. I was stunned, to say the least. I clenched my jaws as I prayed, asking God to seal my mouth so nothing negative would be said.

Within minutes, Carmen entered the stage and I was caught up in the presence of God flowing through this anointed man of God. God was definitely in the house and used Carmen's music and testimonies to display His love and power. Many people made the decision to ask Christ into their lives when Carmen gave an invitation.

When the concert finished, I stayed in my pew knowing I'd have to wait for Mike to finish with security. After fifteen minutes, I decided to head toward the foyer to find him. As I turned around to gather my items, I was surprised to see the young man and his family sitting behind me. I smiled to each of them and told them goodbye as I started to walk away from my seat. Just as I was leaving, the young man stood up and said in a callous, indifferent tone, "Sorry." His mother must have asked him to apologize. Nonetheless, he did make an effort, which I eagerly accepted. After he apologized, I started to leave, but then it happened....

I felt the urge to go back and talk to the young man.

I knew the Holy Spirit was prompting me to share Jesus with him. It frightened me because of the situation I had just experienced with the young man, but I knew, without any doubt, God was telling me to express the love of Jesus and His sacrifice on the cross. God's prompting kept playing over and over in my mind. *"Barbara, tell this man how much I love him."*

Satan, on the other hand, was telling me I should ignore the prompting. He reminded me this was not a nice guy, so he'd probably laugh at me or cuss me out again. Satan urged me to walk away and forget it. There was a war going on inside me, but I remembered Julie's commitment to no longer say *no* to God's promptings, and I chose to do the same. I prayed for wisdom and strength, and I took the plunge. I had no idea what to say, but I turned back around and introduced myself and asked if he liked the concert.

"It was okay," he replied. "I heard this message before when I was in juvenile detention."

I continued to ask questions and he told me he'd been a member of a gang, and had been in numerous fights with guns pointed at his head several times. "Do you know Jesus Christ?" I asked at one point in the conversation.

"I thought I asked Jesus into my heart, but I never felt changed."

I explained to him the transformation that takes place when Christ enters our hearts. I shared 2 Corinthians 5:17 where it says, *"Therefore, if anyone is in Christ, he is a new creation: the old has gone, the new has come!"*

I spoke about other aspects of being a Christian, and when our conversation ended, I asked, "Do you want to be a part of God's forever family?"

"I'll have to think about it."

I decided to try to find Mike or Myron so they could talk with him man to man, so I said, "I'll be leaving in about fifteen minutes, but let me find my husband first."

After looking everywhere, not able to locate either of them, I headed back to the sanctuary. The young man and his family were still sitting in the pew, the only ones in the sanctuary.

The young man looked like he was fighting an inner battle. He was fidgeting and wringing his hands, and had a troubled expression on his face. As I gathered the items I left in the pew, I asked him, "Have you thought more about being a part of God's family?"

"I have, but I'm not sure yet."

"Okay. Well, God bless you. It was nice to meet you all," I said my good-byes and began to walk away.

When I did, he quickly stood up and asked, "Will you pray with me?"

I took him into another room and he shared more of the story of his troubled youth, and then he asked Jesus to forgive him and be Lord of his life. Immediately after he prayed, his countenance changed. He was joyful, smiling and happy. He felt the burden of his sin lift off his heart and he knew he was changed.

"God has transformed and changed you, and now it is your mission to tell your family and friends about this salvation and forgiveness you have received," I said.

As we were leaving, his family told me they brought him to the concert in the hope he would find Jesus. They were shocked when he first cussed at me, and they were surprised when I didn't retaliate. It made an impression on all of them.

"It was all Jesus, sealing my mouth so that He could open my heart to someone who needed His love."

Barbara's fear level before the interaction: 7*

During the interaction: 3 or 4

*Fear Rating: 10 is extremely nervous or fearful and 0 is not nervous or fearful at all

KARIS JOHNSTON

Karis is one of my founding board members for Crazy About You Ministries because of her passion to see God move in power and love wherever she goes. She worked as a nurse before having children, but is now a fulltime home school mother. She is an inspiration to everyone she meets.

~Healing in Sporting Goods~

My four young children were at home with their dad as I headed to Walmart. *I haven't prayed for anyone at Walmart for some time, Lord, but I want to be a blessing, so please make it simple and easy.*

I saw a good friend from church in the parking lot and we briefly chatted, encouraging each other as we praised God for His goodness in our lives. When we finished visiting, I headed into the store.

While I was in the produce section, I bumped into another friend whose daughter was recently diagnosed with Graves' disease.

"Can I pray for her right now?" I asked. She seemed a little uncomfortable praying in public, but she agreed, so I made it quick. "I declare health and healing, and I bind this disease in Jesus' name...." When I finished praying, I gave her a hug and we both carried on with our shopping.

When I was near sporting goods, I noticed a man driving an electric cart who had two preteen children with him. I almost passed him by, but I allowed God to be bigger than my discomfort. I turned down the camping aisle and walked toward them.

"How are you?" I asked.

"We're all right," he responded.

One of his kids was dressed in a baseball uniform, so I struck up a conversation about his kids' sports activities. We switched from talking about his kids' sports to the church that he attended. It was easy to converse with him because he was very friendly and I discovered we both love Jesus.

"Why are you in an electric cart?" I asked.

"I hurt my knee playing sports many years ago, and now the pain is so excruciating that it's hard to walk. I may need surgery soon."

"I hurt my knee mountain biking eighteen years ago and had corrective surgery," I said, "but it was still messed up and painful, and didn't work correctly. When Bill Johnson spoke at a conference a few years ago, he prayed for healing for all the people with hurt knees. My knee was immediately healed and I was able to kneel for the first time in many years."

"That's amazing!"

"I enjoy praying for people to be healed, so can I pray for you?"

"Sure."

So right there, in the midst of lanterns and folding chairs, I prayed. "I command healing to this knee, and command every ligament and all the cartilage to line up with the perfect word of God that declares by the stripes of Jesus he is healed!"

The Holy Spirit prompted me, *"Have him test it."* But I was feeling fearful, so I didn't ask. We finished talking and said good-bye. I started to walk away, but as I did, the man stood up and began to bend his knee to check it.

"Is there any improvement?" I turned around and asked.

"Yes. But there's still some pain."

"Can I pray again and lay a hand on your knee?"

"Sure."

"I command the rest of this pain to go in Jesus' name and for there to be complete restoration of movement."

He bent his knee and smiled. "It feels much better!" He took several steps, bending with each step, and his face showed obvious relief at what God had done. "Thank you!"

"Praise God. He is so good!"

When I was paying for my groceries a little while later, he and his kids passed by me and waved—but this time he was walking and the kids were using the cart for a joyride.

Thank You, Jesus, for helping me to speak life and health over one of Your beloved children!

Karis's fear level before the interaction: 3

During the interaction: 0

Asking him to check his injury to see if it's healed: 7

CAMILLE COLLIE

Camille is a long-time friend and sweet lover of Jesus. The story below happened many years ago, but she has been stepping out recently and saying *yes* to God's promptings once again, and she's excited to see how God is using her to encourage others.

❧*Illogical Obedience*❧

I was driving home from church one evening on a dark two-lane highway when I passed a man jogging along the side of the road. I couldn't tell how old he was, but I could definitely tell he was a man. As soon as I passed him, I heard very clearly in my mind, *"Pick him up."*

This can't be God, I thought. *I'm alone in a small car and I'm sure God wouldn't be telling me to pick up a strange man on a dark road late at night. That's not logical.*

I continued to drive on, but a couple minutes later I heard it again. *"Go pick him up."*

Again I thought, *This can't be God*, and I continued driving.

When I came to a stoplight, I heard again, but even more adamantly, *"GO AND PICK HIM UP."*

I finally said, "Okay, God, I'm going to believe I just heard from You, so protect me!" I turned the car around, drove back to where he was, and flung open the passenger door.

A young man stuck his head in the door. "Do you need a ride?" I asked.

"Yes! Can you take me to the 7-11?"

"Sure. Hop in."

"I just dropped my girlfriend off at her house after attending a meeting at our church where my father is the pastor," he said. "I didn't want to admit to my girlfriend that I was about to run out of gas, and sure enough, I ran out shortly after I dropped her off. When I was jogging along the road, I was praying someone would pick me up!"

His comments confirmed that I had indeed heard the voice of God. I dropped him off at the 7-11 so that he could call his brother for help (because this was before cell phones were popular). I drove home amazed at what had just happened, and I was thankful I had been obedient to God's voice even when it seemed illogical.

Camille's fear level before the interaction: 5
During the interaction: 0

RICHELLE BELTRAND

Richelle is our oldest daughter and currently does hair at a salon several days a week. She walks in a lot of love and pushes past her shyness to share Jesus' love with her clients. She is a godly, amazing woman and a blessing in so many ways!

⊱*Too Much Pain to Live*⊰

I am naturally a quiet person, so I am still learning to forget my fears and love people no matter how nervous I am. I do share with people as the Holy Spirit prompts me, but I'm not as intentional or as bold as I'd like to be. I realize, though, that listening for the Holy Spirit's promptings is a daily choice and that I need to make that choice no matter how I feel. People are worth it!

My mom challenged me to ask and expect God to speak through me for someone at work the next day, so I accepted the challenge. Before the day began I had in my head which client it would be, but as I worked with an elderly woman I felt the nudging from Jesus. *"Share My love with her."*

She had been telling me how she had been experiencing incredible pain for months. "I'm ready to leave the earth," she said.

"Do you know Jesus?" I gently asked.

"I've gone to church."

"But do you have Jesus in your heart and life?"

"No," she replied with a little laugh, indicating she didn't know what I meant.

"Jesus loves you and died for your sins so that you could have a relationship with Him. In fact, He's thinking about you right now and told me to tell you."

She shook her head. "It's too late for me. I'm not worthy."

"None of us are worthy," I said. "We all have messed up and need Jesus to forgive us." I continued to talk with her about the gift of eternal life that Jesus died to give her, and that she has only to receive it. I shared other truths of God's love for her.

Since she comes in every week, I had an idea. "If you happen to have a Bible, how about if you read the book of John this week and then we'll talk about it next week?" I asked.

"Okay. I can do that," she said.

Jesus, show me what to say and do to help draw this precious woman to You before she leaves this earth. We never know how much time we have left, and her time seems especially short.

Richelle's fear level before the interaction: 5
During the interaction: 2 or 3

STUART GURNEA

Stuart is one of CAYM's founding board members because of his ability to hear God. He often shares very detailed prophetic words and has seen numerous healings in the U.S. and around the world, yet I love that God still gives him simple impressions and words to touch people's hearts.

⹂Concern in Her Eyes⹌

My wife Nancy and I had company from out of state staying with us. We all went to lunch after church, and I noticed that our waitress was sweet, friendly and helpful. Each time she came to our table I studied her face. She was smiling, but I could see worry below the surface.

What is she concerned about, Lord?

"A relative," the Lord responded to my thoughts.

Before paying our bill and leaving, I spoke with her. "My name is Stuart. What is your name?"

"Maria," she said.

"Are you concerned about a relative?"

"Yes," she said with a questioning look in her eyes as if to ask me how I knew and why I was even interested.

"I'm a Christian and the Lord placed you on my heart. When I sensed your concern, the Lord told me you were concerned about a relative."

Maria began to cry. "My husband has been suffering from liver disease for years. In fact, doctors told him he had only months to live—and that was fifteen years ago. He is getting much worse lately and I'm really worried about him. I'm also concerned about our oldest son who is having trouble finding work and is struggling with depression."

"Can we pray for you and your family right now?"

"Oh, yes, please!"

I grabbed her hands and prayed for healing for her husband, and employment and freedom from depression for her son. "The Lord wants you to know that He is pleased with you, and that your faith and prayers have sustained your husband these many years."

She cried again.

I shared the rest of what I was sensing: "A season of spiritual revival and love for Jesus is coming on your household. Continue to pray for your family and bless them as they come and go. Trust the Lord and expect His hand to move in your home and see what happens."

"Thank you so much!" she said as she hugged us and we said good-bye.

Now that was a good lunch, Lord!

Stuart's fear level before the interaction: 0

During the interaction: 0

DANE EARL

Dane, our son, loves Jesus and ignores his fears in order to pray for people for healing and to share words of prophecy at school and around town. He is an incredible man of God and a lot of fun. (This story happened while he was at Bethel School of Supernatural Ministry in Redding, California a few years ago when he was first starting to listen and obey God's promptings.)

❧*Skateboarder Restored*❧

Unlike some mornings, I woke up with expectation. *Jesus, I love You and I'm eager to see what You'll do today!*

I worked a morning shift at a retail store in the mall, and several hours into the morning I began to get excited because I felt God was going to do something outside the mall after work. When my shift ended, I was tired but expectant. I headed toward the parking lot.

Jesus, who do You want me to share with and pray for today?

I didn't feel anything until I walked outside and saw a young man wearing skater shoes and baggy shorts sitting in front of the mall. I knew in my spirit this was the young man I was supposed to talk with, but fear immediately welled up inside me and I walked right by him. I was at least thirty feet past him when I reminded myself that my fears shouldn't define me, but my ability to overcome my fears is what should define who I am. I fearfully turned back around.

"Hey, man," I said with a sheepish grin as I walked up to him. "I know this might sound weird, but I was wondering if you have lower back pain, knee pain and something hurting in your wrist?" This is often the way I start a conversation. I ask God for a word of knowledge about any physical pain in a person's body.

The young man looked at me with a puzzled expression. "Yes, how did you know that?"

"I love Jesus and I love people, so I try to hear God's voice for what He might be saying for people who He highlights to me. I'm Dane. What is your name?"

"I'm Josh." (Not his real name.)

I began to prophesy life over him. "I see you as a man of strength in your family and a pillar of hope to the people around you. God has given you leadership qualities and He wants to start using that in you. God also wants to restore your relationship with your family. I see you and your dad's relationship being restored in particular."

"Yeah man. This all makes sense."

I could tell he was deeply touched that God knew him and cared about his life. We talked a little longer, and then I asked if I could pray for him and for God to heal him.

"Yes. My wrist is hurting right now. I hurt it not too long ago while I was skateboarding." He pointed to a bulge on his wrist where the broken bone was protruding. Then he pointed to his knee. "I also shattered my knee a few years ago and barely have any kneecap left."

"Jesus radically loves you, Josh, and the Bible says it is God's will to heal people if we just have faith that He can do it. Can I put my hand on your shoulder and pray for your wrist and knee?"

"Yes."

I kept it short as usual, just like Jesus did when He prayed. "Jesus, I command in Your name that all pain be gone in Josh's wrist and in his knee. You said we should pray that God's will be done on earth as it is done in heaven, so I call that reality down to earth and command healing because You paid for Josh's healing." Once I finished praying, I asked, "Is there anything going on in your body?"

"My chest feels hot and the pain is gone in my wrist!"

"When the Holy Spirit comes to heal, sometimes it feels hot," I explained.

He began to move his wrist, and then he started shouting. "The pain is gone and the bone isn't protruding through my skin! That's blankety-blank crazy!"

"God loves you, Josh, and He wants you to know without a shadow of a doubt that He cares about you, man!" He looked at me in unbelief. "How is your knee?"

"It doesn't seem any better."

"If Jesus prayed more than once for someone to be healed in the Bible, then I certainly can, too. Do you mind if I pray again for your knee?" He nodded with excitement, so I put my hand on his knee. "Jesus, I command healing in Your name. All bone be repaired, and I ask for a creative miracle to take place in Josh's knee."

"What the blank!" Josh cussed with excitement. "My knee doesn't hurt and the kneecap is totally normal now! That is blanket-blank-blank crazy. Here—feel it," he said to me.

Sure enough, the kneecap felt totally solid and normal. "Praise God! God doesn't want anyone to be in pain because He loves us." I talked with Josh about receiving Jesus' forgiveness and starting a relationship with God.

"I don't think I'm quite ready right now," he said thoughtfully. We talked a little longer about what it means to live life with God.

"Here's my phone number," I said. "When you're ready, give me a call. Or if you want to just talk or hang out, give me a call."

I was surprised Josh didn't receive Christ right then and there, but I knew God would use this awesome encounter, along with many other encounters, to keep drawing Josh to Himself. *Thank You, Jesus, for helping me ignore my fears so that You could love Josh through me today!*

Dane's fear level before the interaction: 7

During the interaction: 2

Asking him to check his injury to see if it's better: 1

They Pushed Past their Fears

What I love about these stories is that almost everyone had some level of discomfort or fear, but they said *No More No* and chose to push past their fear or discomfort and say *yes* to God's prompting. Once they took the plunge and began talking or helping the person God highlighted to them, they were no longer afraid, or felt only minimal fear. By the end of each interaction, everyone was blessed and excited about being able to take part in delivering God's love gifts.

It's always amazing how fun, uplifting and refreshing it is when we say *yes* to God and obey His leading. *"He who refreshes others will himself be refreshed,"* (Proverbs 11:25).

You, too, can push past your fears and deliver God's gifts of love to your world!

Part 4

Breaking Free from Fear and Apathy

These next three chapters are my favorites because when you fall in love with Jesus, fall in love with people and understand the authority you've been given, your life will be radically transformed. Sins, depression, fear and apathy will dissolve. You'll be so in love with Jesus and so in love with people that you won't care if you look foolish or embarrass yourself. All you'll care about is honoring God with your *yes* and walking in the authority and love He's given you to do His work on the earth.

Chapter 10

Fall in Love with Jesus

I was once again lying in the dark.

The bedroom blinds were closed, my pink mask was covering my eyes and my head was elevated to relieve the pressure. Several weeks earlier I had slipped in my kitchen on a melted ice cube and slammed my head into the wall. All stimuli to the brain—noise, light, touch and motion—still increased my pain and nausea, so here I was in the dark and silence while my family was downstairs making supper.

Since we can communicate with the Lord in our thoughts, He and I were having another sweet conversation. Shortly into our talk, I saw Jesus come and sit on the bed. This wasn't a physical vision, but I saw Him very clearly in my mind's eye. He was wearing khaki pants, a dress shirt and brown shoes. I don't often see Jesus in modern clothes, but since He wore modern clothes when He came to earth 2,000 years ago, it made sense He would have on modern clothes for me. He stretched out on His back beside me on the bed, crossed His arms behind His head and crossed His ankles. He looked very relaxed, and I couldn't help but chuckle at the sight. He turned to look at me and laughed along.

When Jesus and I stopped chuckling, I knew He wanted to talk about what was heavy on my heart, so I jumped right in. *Jesus, I know the Father, Son and Holy Spirit are Three-in-One, but I have a hard time addressing just You or just the Father or just the Holy Spirit. When I'm praying, I rotate between addressing each of You because I don't want to leave anyone out. But I've been feeling lately that this is keeping me from a deeper level of intimacy that You desire to have with me.*

"I want you to look into my eyes," Jesus said as He lifted up on one elbow and turned His face toward me. I gazed directly into His loving eyes as He continued to gently speak. *"If you've seen Me, you've seen the Father. I and the Father are One."* I had read and even taught those same truths from John 14:9 and John 10:30 many times, but spoken from His lips, the beauty and impact of what He was saying rocked my spirit.

Then I saw the Father looking at me through Jesus' eyes. *"It's Me."*

Tears sprang to my eyes with the realization of what He was showing me. When I'm looking at Jesus, I'm looking at the Father.

"This is why I want you to fix your eyes on Jesus," the Father continued. *"When you're talking with Jesus, you're talking with Me—and My Spirit. When you're wrapping your arms around Jesus, you're wrapping your arms around Me. When you're dancing with Jesus, you're dancing with Me. When you're being held by Jesus, you're being held by Me. When you're doing battle against the enemy with Jesus, you're doing battle against the enemy with Me. We are truly One."*

It's hard to describe what happens when a truth you've known your whole life bursts forth with fresh revelation, and the magnitude of that truth settles deep into your spirit. Everything shifts.

I no longer had to talk with all three in equal amounts to be polite. I could talk with the Father or Jesus or the Holy Spirit all day long every day, and I would be talking with all three. I could embrace and focus on one "Person" and no one would be left out.

Fix Your Eyes on Jesus

After this encounter, I took the Father's words seriously and began fixing my eyes on Jesus as it says in Hebrews 12:2. I began picturing Him in my mind's eye and talking with Him "face-to-face" wherever I was. If I was on the couch, I pictured Jesus sitting there with me as we talked. If I was in the kitchen, I pictured Him beside me doing dishes. If I was driving in the car, He was in the passenger seat.

I've talked with the Father, Son and Holy Spirit throughout the day since I was a little girl, but picturing Him in my mind's eye was something I only did sporadically. So as I began this new practice of fixing my eyes on Jesus and picturing Him all day long, I was amazed at the difference it made in how aware I was of His presence and how close I felt to Him. He's always been very near to me and precious beyond words, but this took our relationship to a much deeper level of intimacy.

THE POWER OF "SEEING"

Satan has warped and twisted the concept of visualizing, as he does with everything God has made. But visualizing isn't wrong—it's powerful. Jesus knew the power of *seeing,* which is why He told so many stories. He wanted people to not only hear the truths, but to also see the truths with their mind's eye.

If I mention the story of David and Goliath, you will probably picture young David and huge Goliath without even thinking about it. You were created to picture—to see with the eyes of your heart.

If someone you love had to leave for an extended period of time, you would picture them in your mind's eye when you thought of them or read their letters. Picturing someone you know and love allows you to feel closer to them. Picturing Jesus allows you to feel closer to Him and to fall more deeply in love.

Why Fall in Love with Jesus?

You may be thinking, *Why do I need to fall in love with Jesus? That sounds weird.* If you're a guy it may sound even weirder, so let's establish the fact right away that God is not a sexual being. He created us as sexual beings to become one flesh with our spouse and to reproduce, but He Himself has no need for sexual reproduction. He has no sexual urges or desires whatsoever because He simply speaks a word and is able to create—as He did when He created the world and everything in it.

When Jesus was on the earth, He was fully God and fully man. But even though He had a normal sex drive, He maintained perfection, never having a lustful, inappropriate thought. So when I talk about falling in love with Jesus, it has nothing to do with sexual love. Jesus loves us emotionally, physically and spiritually, just as a mother or father tenderly loves their child. The only difference is that Jesus loves us perfectly and completely.

FALLING IN LOVE IS A GPS CRITERIA

Every package you deliver when you live a *Yes, Lord* lifestyle has to do with Jesus' love. You'll either be directly expressing His love to someone or their gift will be wrapped in His love.

I know a Christian man who had been a believer for thirty-four years, but he struggled to love others and he constantly battled a critical spirit. He was at a conference one weekend, seeking God during worship, when his heart finally opened to receive God's love. He walked away a changed man, and he has continued to grow in his love relationship by spending time in God's presence.

When he was telling me of his experience, he told me, "You can't give what you don't have." He is now able to better love his wife and children with the love that is bubbling up within him by God's Spirit.

Since we work for God's Parcel Service and are the hands, feet and mouth of Jesus on the earth, falling in love with Jesus is essential to our success because we can't give what we don't have.

The Benefits of Falling in Love

THE HOLD OF FEAR WILL BE BROKEN

One of the many benefits of falling in love with Jesus is that your fears will diminish, and eventually disappear, as the reality of His love grows in your heart and mind. *"There is no fear in love. But perfect love drives out fear"* (1 John 4:18). Jesus' love is perfect, so as you envelop yourself in His perfect love, fear will be completely broken from your life—fear of others' opinions, fear of messing up, fear of being rejected and all other fears that keep you from trusting God. You'll be so in love with Jesus that it won't matter what others are thinking or saying about you. All that will matter is that you are loving Him and saying *yes* to His every prompting.

"The one who fears is not made perfect in love" (1 John 4:18), so use fear as your love litmus. If you are experiencing fear of any kind then you haven't been made perfect in love. I know I haven't, because I sometimes feel fear when the Holy Spirit prompts me to say or do things for Him. I've learned to ignore my fears most of the time, but I want to get to the place where I am so completely in love with Jesus that fearful thoughts don't even pop into my mind when

the Holy Spirit prompts me to do something. I want to be so immersed and surrounded in His love that fear can't make its way to my mind or heart.

YOUR ATTITUDES AND ACTIONS WILL CHANGE

When Jesus was asked which commandment was the greatest, Jesus said: *"Love the Lord your God with all your heart and with all your soul and with all your mind and with all your strength"* (Mark 12:30). Why? Because Jesus knows God's love—His love—changes everything. He knows if you make it your goal to fall in love with Him, and love Him with every part of your being, then your every word, action and attitude will be changed by that love.

We see this same principle in a romance. When a man and woman fall in love, they rarely need to be told how to act. Their love for each other automatically makes them want to do kind things and express their love in their actions and words. Why? Because they are love-struck.

The same is true with Jesus. If you regularly spend time in His presence, you will become love-struck and will ache to please Him in all you do. Your behaviors will automatically begin to change from the inside out. Jesus said, *"If you love me, you will obey what I command"* (John 14:15). The result of loving Jesus is that you will obey His commands because your heart's desire will be to delight His heart in the same way He delights yours. When you fall in love with Jesus you will experience victory over sins that have plagued you for years; victory over lies of the enemy that have kept you depressed and bound; and victory over fear and apathy that has kept you from being the mighty warrior God has called you to be.

So if your heart's desire is to change, don't focus on your sin. Focus on Jesus and allow His love to make the changes.

GOD WILL SHOW YOU MORE OF HIMSELF

Another benefit of falling in love with Jesus is that He will show you more of Himself. *"He who loves me will be loved by my Father, and I too will love him and show myself to him"* (John 14:21). Wow! What a privilege and treasure to be shown more of the mind and heart of God. As you make the effort to love Him and draw near to Him, He will draw near to you (see James 4:8).

The gifts of the Spirit aren't earned, but imagine the depth of insight and revelation added to those gifts by you, a GPS employee who is in love with Jesus, because you have been shown more of the heart of God. Imagine how blessed people will be because of those added insights and revelations.

I often hear Christians pray for *more* of God, and I've done it myself many times, but according to Jesus, the ball is in our court. The *more* is a result of spending time with Him. As we daily fall in love with Jesus, He will show us more of Himself. God can send lightning bolts of power, revelation and love, and He sometimes does, transforming people in an instant. But He prefers that we stay in His presence and are daily transformed by His love. Why? Because He is thrilled to hang out with us! He didn't create us to leave us alone, expecting us to do life on our own. He created us to walk with Him and be His dear children and friends.

YOU WILL RECEIVE WHAT YOU ASK FOR

Can you imagine being so in love with Jesus, so completely one with Him and His words, that everything your heart wishes for is what God's heart wishes for? That's what Jesus said in John 15:7-8: *"If you remain* [abide, live] *in me and my words remain* [abide, live] *in you, ask whatever you wish, and it will be given you. This is to my Father's glory, that you may bear much fruit, showing yourselves to be my disciples"* (John 15:7-8). Your heart won't be wrapped up in thoughts of the newest techno gadgets, fancy cars, clothes or houses. Your heart will be completely wrapped up in God's love.

Jesus was given what He asked for when He was on the earth because He was One with the Father. Even when Jesus grappled in the Garden of Gethsemane, counting the cost of taking the sins of the world upon His body, He submitted to the Father's love, knowing that He, as God in the flesh, had to pay the price for the world to be redeemed.

The Father wants this same oneness with us. Jesus said, *"I am in my Father, and you are in me, and I am in You"* (John 14:20). Jesus said if we live in His love and His words live in us, whatever we ask will be given to us. Since this promise is hard to imagine, let's look at John 15:7 more closely, especially the part about His words living in us.

I used to think when Jesus said *"If...my words remain* [abide, live] *in you"* that He was encouraging us to memorize the Bible, but I don't believe Bible memory was His main emphasis in making this statement. I believe Jesus was talking more about our *response* to His words—His words from the Bible and His words spoken to our hearts.

. How we respond to Jesus' words determines whether those words will live or die in us. If we believe His promises and let them become the truth we live by (even when we can't see them in the natural), and if we say *yes* to His commands and promptings, doing what He asks, then His words will stay alive in us. Jesus' words will accomplish what He intended and will produce incredible fruit in our lives and others' lives because *"the word of God is living and active"* (Hebrews 4:12).

If we say *no* to Jesus' promises and commands, and don't believe or obey them, they are no longer abiding and living. They will die in us and will accomplish nothing.

Look at these scenarios:

Jesus encouraged Joe to walk in patience and forgiveness with a difficult person at work, but Joe ignored Jesus and became angry instead. Those words from Jesus died and became fruitless because Joe ignored them.

The Father prompted Sue to turn off her TV one evening and spend time worshipping Him, allowing Him to minister peace to her troubled spirit. But Sue ignored the Father and left the TV on. As a result, Sue missed the peace and joy God wanted to breathe into her spirit that evening, and His words to her died.

The Holy Spirit whispered to Fred to slow down at the grocery store so that He could give Fred a word of knowledge for the man shopping nearby. But Fred didn't believe God's promise that God's sheep (God's children) can hear His voice, so Fred said *no* and walked past the man. The Holy

Spirit's words died and the man Fred was supposed to talk with missed an interaction with God that was meant to dramatically alter his life.

Sadly, we've all said *no* to Jesus. When we say *no,* we are killing His words and not allowing them to live and bear fruit.

Even as I'm typing this section, Jesus prompted me to give away all the delicious brisket that has been slow cooking in my crock pot for eighteen hours. The brisket was on sale this week, so my plan had been to give some of it to Richelle, Luke and Ryder since they are arriving home from a ten-day vacation, and then for Ron, Dane and I to eat the rest of it for several days.

When the prompting came to give most of it to our neighbors who are moving tomorrow, and the rest to Richelle and Luke, it took me several minutes to say *yes.* Jesus was not asking me to share it, but to give it all away. I thought of several reasons why our neighbors probably didn't need it and already had their food taken care of for this evening and tomorrow. But I knew this wasn't about them having enough food. This was about God wanting to love them.

My eyes filled with tears as I again felt the tenderness of God for this dear family who had suffered so much loss this past year. "Yes, Lord! I would be honored to give all of my brisket away to be Your arms of love for them."

If I had said *no* and reasoned myself out of obeying Jesus' prompting, then His words to me would have died and been fruitless. But because I said *yes,* His words were able to abide and live, and to bear fruit for my neighbors.

It's not enough to read and memorize the Bible, or listen for God's words to our thoughts. Those words aren't living, remaining or abiding in us until we actually *believe* and *obey* them.

In the light of this truth, let's look at John 15:7 again: *"If you remain [abide, live] in me and my words remain [abide, live] in you, ask whatever you wish, and it will be given you."* If we live in Jesus' love with our every word and action flowing from His love, and if we allow His words to *live* in us, believing His promises and saying *yes* to what He asks us to do, then we will get what we ask for. We will receive detailed words of prophecy, sick people will be healed, those oppressed by demons will be set free and our needs and others' needs will be met. We'll have the confidence to operate in the supernatural life Jesus meant for us to live, and many will come to Jesus as a result.

GOD WILL BLESS YOUR SOCKS OFF

God also responds to your love by blessing your socks off. *"'No eye has seen, no ear has heard, no mind has conceived what God has prepared for those who love him'—but God has revealed it to us by His Spirit"* (1 Corinthians 2:9-10).

This doesn't mean you won't have trials and hard times. Jesus said, *"In this world you will have trouble"* (John 16:33). But in the midst of all the junk Satan and the world will dish out, you will see God move in power and do incredible things in and through you no matter what attacks come your way. You are promised that *"God causes all things to work together for good to those who love God, to those who are called according to His purpose"* (Romans 8:28). Can you think of many greater blessings than having all things work together for good in your life? I can't!

Practical Ideas for Intimacy

I consider this chapter to be the most important chapter in this book. Not only because intimacy with God will free you from your fears so that you can share His love and truth with strangers, friends and family, but because the whole point of your existence is to have a love relationship with God. You were created to be loved by God and to love Him in return. I've listed fourteen ideas to help you fall in love with God—with the Father, Jesus and the Holy Spirit—and my prayer is that you will refer back to this section regularly and come up with many other ideas of your own.

Please don't make these suggestions a type of law for yourself so that you feel guilty if you aren't doing all of them or any of them. I have days where I'm doing a number of them, and days where I'm only doing a few. This isn't about earning your way to God by checking off a daily list of dos and don'ts. He already loves you and you are already righteous in His sight, so there is nothing to earn.

These are meant to be fun ways to spend more time in His presence in the midst of your daily routine so that you can enjoy each other.

#1: PICTURE JESUS

As I mentioned earlier, picturing Jesus will take you to new levels of intimacy. You can picture Jesus doing daily tasks with you, or doing activities alongside you that speak love and healing to your spirit. For example, picture yourself sitting in His lap, walking together, resting by a river, having fun wrestling, hunting together and any other activities that speak love and intimacy to you.

This whole concept might sound strange, but Jesus knew the importance of our awareness of His presence. We know this because the last words Jesus spoke before He ascended to heaven were about His presence: *"I am with you always, to the very end of the age"* (Matthew 28:20). He is with you all the time, so enjoy picturing Him as your best friend, because that's what He is!

#2: SAY "I LOVE YOU, JESUS"

As soon as your eyes open in the morning, a number of times throughout the day, and before you fall asleep at night, tell Jesus you love Him. Saying, "I love You, Jesus," whether out loud or in your head, will turn your affections back to His heart and will awaken your senses to His presence and love for you.

I'm always amazed at the impact these words have on me no matter what issues or challenges are swirling around me. If I'm feeling attacked, alone, discouraged or stressed, or if I'm feeling great, telling Jesus, "I love You" lifts my spirits and connects me to Him.

I can't emphasize enough how much this one simple act, done throughout the day, can transform your walk with Jesus and your outlook on life.

#3: SHARE TWO-WAY CONVERSATIONS

Once you say, "I love You, Jesus," let His response form in your mind and allow Him to speak to your thoughts.

As soon as I open my eyes, a morning conversation may sound like this:

"Good morning, Jesus. I love You!"

"Good morning, dear Julie. I love you, too!"

"Thank you for the good night's sleep—for the seven hours I got anyway." We both chuckle at this because getting to bed on time is usually a struggle for me. "Help me get to sleep sooner tonight."

"You're doing much better, so don't be discouraged," Jesus sweetly responds.

"Thanks for the encouragement! Your grace and patience inspire me to keep growing."

The conversation can turn any number of directions, but my main goal is to step into His love and enjoy being with Jesus as we converse back and forth. No one likes being in a one-way conversation—especially not Jesus. He wants us to hear His heart as much as He wants to hear ours.

#4: WRITE DOWN HIS WORDS TO YOU

One of the best ways to remember Jesus' words to you is to write them down in some type of journal. I try to sit down three-to-four times per week and type what Jesus speaks to my thoughts at that moment. I've only been doing this for a few years, and some weeks I forget all together, but on the days I do remember, it's a tremendous blessing. I'm no longer just reporting things that Jesus said to me in my own words, but I literally type as He speaks to my thoughts.

Mark Virkler has done an excellent, in-depth teaching on this concept in a DVD set and book entitled *Four Keys to Hearing God's Voice.*[13] He answers numerous questions for those still learning to trust that God is speaking to His children, and he gives practical advice such as having someone you trust read what you write in the beginning to see if it sounds like God's voice.

How honored the Lord must be when we not only listen to His voice, but we take the time to write down His words of love, wisdom and insight so that we can treasure them now and in the future.

#5: IMMERSE YOURSELF IN THE BIBLE

Speaking of treasuring God's words to us, the Holy Spirit inspired numerous people in the past to write down His words of wisdom, love and revelation, and they are compiled in the Bible. Immersing yourself in the Bible will transform your life and your love relationship more than you can imagine. You don't need formal Bible studies to be transformed (although some of those can be wonderful). Simply ask the Holy Spirit to open your eyes and show you His character and love as you read.

Don't read for information, but for inspiration. Ask the Holy Spirit to apply what you read to your life. Every time you read, you'll discover new insights, so His Word never gets boring. If you are bored, use your authority to break off the lies and blinders of the enemy that try to keep you from experiencing the amazing revelation, delight and wonder found in God's Word.

The more voraciously you read, study and meditate, the more your life will be transformed and the more truth you'll have to offer your world as you deliver gifts on your GPS route. I'm amazed how the Holy Spirit brings to mind certain verses or insights at just the right time because I've made reading the Bible a priority in my life.

Just be careful not to let the devil condemn you on the days you don't read the Bible. Simply love on Jesus, receive His love and enjoy His presence. I used to feel tremendous guilt if I didn't read the Bible every day, and it hurt my relationship with the Lord more than I recognized at the time. Once I realized Jesus hadn't set up a New Testament Bible Reading Law, and that I can simply read out of love and a desire for more of Him rather than out of obligation, then I wanted to read even more.

Modern technology also makes it easy for you to listen to the Bible while you get dressed, exercise, drive, do yard work, cook or relax on the couch. You won't have as much time to stop and ponder sections, but you'll pick up things you might not catch when you're reading. Listening to God's love and truth will help you tune in to God's heart and get you properly focused throughout the day.

The more time you spend reading and listening to God's Words of truth and love, the more you'll be transformed without even trying.

#6: KEEP TALKING

First Thessalonians 5:17 (NKJV) says, *"Pray without ceasing."* It's amazing to me that Jesus wants to talk with us all day long. I love my kids tremendously and have always enjoyed conversations with them (unless they were whining, complaining or fighting), but even with all the love I feel for them, I don't want to talk to them without ceasing (and I'm sure they don't want to talk to me without ceasing). We all need breaks.

But Jesus' love is far beyond our human love and He truly wants to talk with us without ceasing. Even though Jesus is busy running the universe, He wants to constantly converse with you and me.

From the time you open your eyes in the morning until you fall asleep at night, your conversation with Jesus never has to end. It can just have short pauses. You can be in and out of talking with Him all day long as things come to mind and as your heart thanks Him for all His love and blessings.

#7: DON'T PRAY A LIST

I used to pray from a list, thinking the more times I mentioned something to the Lord, the more chance I had that He would give me what I wanted. I suppose I thought of it as a raffle, and the more tickets I bought, the more opportunity I had of winning.

But when I pictured one of my kids coming to me every day with a list of all the things they wanted me to do for them, I could no longer bring myself to come to my Father in that way. I'm not saying lists are wrong, but I wasn't able to grow in intimacy until I laid down my lists and focused on relationship rather than requests.

I still present my requests to God as the Holy Spirit brings them to mind, but then I trust God with those requests. Jesus said, *"The Father knows what you need before you ask Him"* (Matthew 6:8), so we don't have to mention every day what He already knows. When the Holy Spirit reminds me to pray about an issue then I gladly pray, but I believe God is most honored when I have faith that He is taking care of the issue and I can release it into His care and wisdom.

There will be times of intercession when the Holy Spirit will remind you often to pray for a particular person or situation as He asks you to do battle in the heavenlies against the works of the devil. But even when you are prompted to pray often, make sure to pray in faith—not fear. Philippians 4:6 says, *"Do not be anxious about anything, but in everything, by prayer and petition, with thanksgiving, present your requests to God."* God doesn't want you to pray because you're worried, but because you have faith that He will take care of the outcome. Pray when He prompts you to pray, and then release the outcome into His capable hands, trusting Him with the results.

#8: ALLOW GOD TO PRAY THROUGH YOU

Wouldn't it be awesome to pray in such a way that you knew your prayers were directly from the Father's heart and you were praying His will?

Amazingly, God did provide a way for you to do just that when He offered the gift of praying in another language (also called the gift of tongues). Once you open your heart to receive this gift, you have the privilege of praying the Father's heart any time you choose—while getting ready for the day, driving in the car, cooking, cleaning, doing yard work—anytime.

I sometimes forget to pray in my prayer language, but when I do remember, my intimacy with Jesus soars as His Spirit prays through me.

#9: GIVE UP DISTRACTIONS AND FOOD

Fasting is another powerful way to fall in love with Jesus. Fasting sets aside food or distractions (or both) for a period of time so that your heart can more fully focus on Jesus. Giving up food, TV, Internet and any number of distractions helps you turn your eyes off those things and onto Jesus.

You're not trying to twist God's arm and impress Him with your sacrifice so that He'll do what you want and answer your prayers. You're trying to remove distractions, and break the hold of those distractions so that you can see Jesus more clearly and be more in love with Him than with those other things. Philippians 3:8-9 says, *"I consider everything a loss compared to the surpassing greatness of knowing Christ Jesus my Lord, for whose sake I have lost all things. I consider them rubbish, that I may gain Christ and be found in Him...."*

If you've never fasted food, start small and skip one or two meals. Then slowly increase the meals you skip as your love for Jesus becomes greater than your love for food. It's hard, but you'll be blessed! (Remember to consult with your doctor before fasting.)

#10: DELIGHT IN JESUS

"Delight yourself in the Lord and He will give you the desires of your heart" (Psalm 37:4). This is the best way to have your prayer needs met. Simply delight in the Lord. Bask in His love for you and in your love for Him.

Here are a few ideas for delighting:

Laugh with Jesus

Laugh together. Share silly parts of your day, talk about your embarrassing moments, discuss the latest joke you heard. Appreciate with Jesus the humor and fun happening around you wherever you look.

God is completely joyful and peaceful, so He is incredibly happy. If you love to laugh and have fun, imagine how much He loves to laugh and have fun! So find out what He's laughing about and laugh with Him. Then share what's making you laugh so that He can laugh with you.

When my alarm went off recently, I woke up exhausted, but I immediately began loving Jesus and allowing Him to love me. After several minutes of conversation, I jokingly asked, "Can you please roll me off the bed?" Picturing Him rolling me off the bed onto the floor made me burst into laughter, and He laughed along.

Play with Jesus

What's your favorite activity? Is it golf, horseback riding, working out, playing a sport, reading a good book or watching movies? Whatever it is, do it with Jesus and enjoy it together. Talk with Him in your thoughts or out loud. When I'm swimming laps or jogging, I invite Jesus along, and we talk and laugh to make the workout more enjoyable. When I'm watching a DVD, I often talk with Him about my love for Him or about what's going on in the movie. He rolls His eyes with me at the corny parts, laughs with me at the funny parts and smiles at me when I cry over the emotional parts.

God gave us our desire to play and have fun because that's the way He is. He isn't the least bit boring. He is the creator and initiator of fun, so join in the fun with Him!

Cry with Jesus

Rather than turning to self-pity, hopelessness or anger, delight in Jesus by turning to Him in crisis. Jesus loves you and He is honored when you come to Him with your pain so that He can lovingly wipe away your tears. He knows life is hard: People can be difficult, circumstances can feel overwhelming and demons attack with their lies every chance they get. Allow Jesus to wrap His arms around you and remind you that none of these challenges are bigger than He is. He's got your back and He'll take care of you in the midst of the storm.

Sometimes when I am feeling deeply hurt by people or situations, I'll lie on my stomach and ask Jesus to come and lie on top of me, shielding me from all attacks and absorbing His healing love into my body, mind and spirit. This picture is similar to the picture written by the Psalmist in Psalm 91:4. *"He will cover you with His feathers, and under His wings you will find refuge; His faithfulness will be your shield and rampart."* Picturing Jesus' body covering mine allows me to feel Him as my refuge—my safe place. The intensity of His love immediately begins healing my pain and gives me renewed confidence that I am safe up high on the "castle" walls (the rampart) and protected by His all-powerful shield—His body. It's incredible how loved and healed I feel as I delight in Jesus in the midst of my pain.

#11: *LIVE IN AN ATTITUDE OF GRATITUDE AND PRAISE*

Choose to be grateful in every situation. If a co-worker or classmate is being mean, be grateful for the growth you'll experience by responding in love instead of anger. If your spouse or a close friend is being insensitive or harsh, thank Jesus that He is always thoughtful and kind, and ask Him to flow that kindness through you. If your child is being willful and disobedient, be grateful for God's grace and the fruit of patience growing in your life as you choose to discipline in love. If you're overwhelmed at your job or school or with the never-ending chores at home, be grateful for the perseverance the Holy Spirit will teach you when you choose to hang in there and not give up.

An important key to growing in intimacy with Jesus is to spend every day in an attitude of gratitude and praise. *"Enter His gates with thanksgiving and His courts with praise"* (Psalm 100:4). David sang in Psalm 95:2, *"Let us come before Him with thanksgiving."* Even the simple comment, "Thank you, Jesus, for the sunshine" can soften your heart and tune your mind and spirit into the Lord's presence.

As a believer, the Lord is always with you, but if you aren't tuned in to His goodness with a listening, grateful spirit, then it's like being beside a radio that isn't turned on. It's there, but you're missing all the benefits of its presence in your life.

Satan knows that being tuned in to God's goodness and living with a grateful spirit will tenderize your heart and allow you to feel Jesus' love no matter what is happening around you. That's why Satan and his demons work overtime to whisper their lies in your ear, getting you tuned out and griping at every difficulty or inconvenience—while driving in traffic, doing piles of dishes or dealing with irritating people. They know negativity will quickly pull your heart away from intimacy with Jesus.

So if you want to defeat Satan and his demonic forces, and if you want to fall madly in love with Jesus, choose to stay in an attitude of gratitude and praise no matter what's happening around you. *"In everything give thanks; for this is God's will for you in Christ Jesus"* (1 Thessalonians 5:18 NASB).

#12: WORSHIP JESUS AT HOME

It's important to live in an attitude of worship and praise all day long, but it's also helpful to set aside time to stop all your activity and simply worship Jesus. Worship in silence or turn on a worship CD from Jesus Culture, Misty Edwards, Bryan and Katie Torwalt or others who know how to sing *to* Jesus rather than just *about* Jesus. Sit on the couch, get on your knees, lay prostrate on the floor or walk around the room. Sing, pray, dance or rest quietly before the Lord, soaking in His love. Tell Him how much you love Him and receive His love for you. Worship Him with your expressions of honor and praise, appreciating His kindness, goodness, faithfulness, gentleness and all the other wonders of His love. Allow His love to seep into your mind and spirit, bringing refreshing and renewal.

#13: WORSHIP WITH TOTAL ABANDON—EVEN PUBLICLY

If you want to fall in love with Jesus and speed up the process of becoming free from fear, then worship Jesus with total abandon— even publicly. Don't put on a show to impress people, but say *yes* to the Holy Spirit's promptings. If you are worshiping at church and the Holy Spirit prompts you to raise your hands—then raise your hands. If He prompts you to kneel—then kneel. If He prompts you to dance a tender, slow dance or a jig of joy—then dance. If He prompts you to fall on your face—then fall.

Each of these physical acts is symbolic of the position of your heart in the same way baptism is symbolic of the position of your heart. Just as baptism is a humble sign of total surrender to God's leadership in your life, raising your hands, kneeling, dancing and lying prostrate before the Lord are all signs—to God, Satan, your-self and the world—that you are humbly surrendering every part of your being to God's love and God's will on a daily basis.

King David humbly worshiped with total abandon because He loved and honored the Lord more than he loved and honored his reputation. Second Samuel 6:14 says David *"danced before the Lord with all his might"* because he was thrilled to have the ark of God—a representation of God's presence—back in Jerusalem.

David laid aside his royal robes and was *"leaping and dancing be-fore the Lord"* unashamedly (verse 16). He didn't care who saw him or what they thought because all he was focused on was God com-ing to stay with them. David's wife, Michal, wasn't in love with God, so David's actions embarrassed her. Her pride caused her to despise David for his open display of affection to God. When she confronted David, his response was: *"I will celebrate before the Lord, I will become even more undignified than this, and I will be humiliated in my own eyes"* (verses 21-22).

It was this passionate love for God that gave David the confi-dence to not only worship freely, but to kill nine-foot Goliath with only a sling and a stone. It's this passionate love for Jesus that will give you the confidence to not only worship with abandon, but to conquer your Goliaths and to fearlessly share God's love with your world!

#14: SAY "YES" TO GOD'S PROMPTINGS

This whole book is about saying yes to God's promptings, but did you know that one of the incredible results of saying *yes* instead of *no* to God's promptings is that you will fall more deeply in love with Jesus? I'm amazed how my love relationship deepened with the Lord once I chose to no longer say *no* to His promptings. Philemon verse 6 is true: *"I pray that you may be active in sharing your faith, so that you will have a full understanding of every good thing we have in Christ."* Every time you express God's love to your world, you yourself are reminded of God's goodness. Every time you are reminded of His goodness and see His goodness in action as you pass out His gifts, you can't help but fall more deeply in love with Him.

So go for it. Trust God and say *yes* to His promptings. Then watch yourself fall head over heels in love with Jesus.

Chapter Highlights and Application

Fix Your Eyes on Jesus: Picture Jesus doing life with you (because He is) and continually tell Him you love Him. Fixing your focus on Jesus rather than what is happening around you will cause your intimacy with Him to soar to new levels.

When I picture Jesus, I like to picture the painting of Him that was drawn by Akiane Kramarik.[14] She had visions of Jesus and painted Him when she was eight years old. When Colton Burpo,[15] who was taken to heaven at age four, saw Akiane's painting of Jesus, he told his parents that was what Jesus looked like. You can see her painting, "Prince of Peace" on my website and on Akiane's site. Even if her painting wasn't perfectly accurate, what's important is that you have your eyes and heart fixed on Jesus (see Hebrews 12:2).

Make Falling in Love with Jesus Your Only Goal: James 4:8 says that if you draw near to God, He will draw near to you. Guess what God's nearness does? It changes you. When you make falling in love with Jesus your only goal, His presence takes care of the rest. You don't have to work on your anger, lust, laziness, pride, depression, critical spirit and on and on. When your only goal is to fall in love with Jesus and immerse yourself in Him, then those things will automatically change in His presence as you yield to Him. In His presence is fullness of joy, peace, purity, love, grace, compassion, kindness, forgiveness and every good thing. If that's the life you want, and the person you want to be for others, then set aside your distractions and spend your days with Jesus.

Practice Saying "No More 'No', Lord" at Church: Honoring God in church with obedient, fearless worship is a tremendous first step in freeing yourself from fear of man and loving God more than your reputation. Ask the Holy Spirit to lead you in worship that honors His heart, and then obey His promptings to raise your hands, kneel, lay prostrate or dance. He will direct you in a way that is sensitive, but not afraid, of those around you. (It's a good idea to check with your worship leader and/or your pastor if this is not normal in your church. You want to honor their leadership. If they don't agree with David and the need to worship God with all your might, then ask God for wisdom and direction in His next step for you.)

Anytime you're at a church service, ask God to highlight someone who needs to hear words of love from God's heart. During worship or once the service is over, go to that person and ask if you can practice hearing God's voice by sharing some words for them. If you aren't hearing anything in particular, then tell the person that God highlighted them to you, and ask how you can pray for them. Church is a perfect place to listen expectantly and begin saying *yes* to God's promptings because you'll inspire others to listen, and because they'll kindly help you grow if you mess up.

Chapter 11

Fall in Love with People

Several years before I made the plunge to say *No More No* to God's promptings, I was desperately crying out to God for help:

How do I overcome my fear and love people more than I love my reputation?

How do I overcome my apathy and care more about others than myself?

God spoke to my heart:
"Pray silently for people wherever you go."

That sounded simple—almost too simple—but I determined to give it a try. The next time I headed out on errands, I began praying silently as my van pulled out of the driveway and I drove down our street. *Lord, bless our neighbors. I know You've been expressing Your love to them their whole lives, so continue to pour out Your incredible love on them even right now.*

I drove around the corner and saw a young man carrying a backpack walking home from school. *Holy Spirit, move in that young man's heart. Help him come to know You as his Savior and Lord if he doesn't already have a relationship with You. Give him the courage not to follow the crowd, but to follow You.*

I made a few more turns and came to a long stoplight. *Holy Spir-*

it, You love the people in the car in front of me. You care about every detail in their lives and You know every time a hair falls from their heads. Open the eyes of their hearts to see their need for forgiveness so they can spend now and eternity in Your presence. Bring people into their lives who can express Your love and truth.

The light changed, and after a few more turns I was at the grocery store. I walked inside, grabbed a cart, and headed to the produce department. As I passed people, I continued to pray in my thoughts. *Father, bless this elderly gentleman who looks bent over with arthritis. Show Him Your healing power. And bless this mother who has three little children making demands on her. Give her wisdom in raising them. Express Your love to her heart and renew her strength. And help this middle-aged woman to know she's not alone. You are there for her.*

As I continued to pray that day, I realized my attitude was shifting in several ways. I felt love growing in my heart for people, and I felt my mood lifting. I'd had the usual parenting challenges that morning, and had been a little grumpy and overwhelmed. But as I prayed for God's love to invade people's hearts, His love further invaded mine. Within a short time, I felt peaceful and lighthearted.

Wow, Jesus! This is awesome. Thanks!

I kept it up, and within a few months of praying for people wherever I went, my love and concern for people increased. My connection with them deepened and my compassion grew.

Amazingly, this simple act of praying God's love and truth on everyone around me was dissolving my fears. My love *for* people became greater than my fear *of* people. My concern for *them* became greater than my concern for *me.*

Another huge benefit of praying for people was that I fell even more deeply in love with Jesus. Every time I prayed for someone, I was entering Jesus' presence and spending time with Him, so I couldn't help but fall more in love.

I never would have dreamed these two simple things—falling in love with Jesus and praying for people—could so transform my life, but they did. My love for Jesus and my love for people began to consume my heart until I was able to ignore the traces of fear and apathy still left, and love people no matter the cost.

I quit being a part-time follower of Jesus, only saying *yes* to His promptings when it was convenient or not too scary, and I finally took up my cross and said *No More No!* I became a fulltime employee with God's Parcel Service and began sharing words of love, wisdom, knowledge and prophecy from the Father's heart, and praying with people for healing or other needs as the Holy Spirit led me.

I haven't done it perfectly, but now, over three-and-a-half years later, I've probably expressed God's love and shared His gifts one-on-one with well over 1,000 people (figuring 6 people per week, which is a low estimate). That's awesome! That's God!

Thoughts and Attitudes Will Change

Praying for people wherever you go is truly life transforming. Your thoughts and attitudes toward people and situations will automatically begin to change. When you're sitting at a long stoplight, you won't be irritated about the wait because you'll be focused on praying for the people around you. When someone cuts you off on the highway, you won't get angry because you'll be praying God's love floods their heart. When a waitress speaks rudely, you won't snap back because compassion will grow in your heart as you pray blessings over her life. When a family member or friend hurts you, you won't hold on to offense and bitterness, because you'll quickly forgive and receive healing from God's heart.

When your flesh does rise up in anger or irritation, as mine still does at times, you can immediately fix your eyes on Jesus, ask Him to pour out His love and blessings on everyone involved, and allow His love to soften your heart.

Even as I'm working on this section, I got very irritated with Ron one morning about something he'd been doing that was hurting my feelings. I didn't yell, but my tone was highly irritated as I pointed out again what was going on. My anger didn't make it easy for Ron to respond in love, so nothing was resolved. I accepted the devil's lies that I was justified in my anger and that self-pity was appropriate in this situation, and a wall of offense went up in my heart. We ate breakfast with minimal eye contact and almost no conversation.

After Ron left for work, I knew I needed to release my anger and allow the Holy Spirit to heal my pain. *I'm sorry, Lord. Help me walk in Your love. I know the fastest way to step back into love and for-giveness is to bless Ron, so please bless Ron in every way today. Help him feel Your love for him and know how special he is to You. Thank You for him and all the wonderful things he does.*

As I continued to pray blessings over him throughout the day, my heart softened. I still felt about ten percent offended when Ron came home, but I kept praying and focusing on Jesus' amazing love for me and for Ron. The following morning Ron indicated he was willing to change the hurtful behavior, and by that evening I real-ized I was completely healed and the wall of offense was gone. I knew even if Ron hadn't offered to change, that God's love still would have healed my heart because I've seen God do it countless times in our marriage and in other relationships. God's love and forgiveness are powerful.

As you begin to pray for people wherever you go around town, don't forget to pray for your family and friends, too. Pray they'll know the tenderness of God's love for them and that God's love will explode in their hearts. Pray that your words and actions will be used by God to express His incredible love for them.

As you intercede for them—not praying they'll change, but praying they'll feel loved and be blessed—you'll see your own atti-tude toward them improve dramatically. It's impossible to stay mad or hold bitterness against someone when you are praying God will bless and honor them.

Do Love

Another great way to grow your love for people is to *do* love. Be intentional in your actions. *"But those who plan what is good find love and faithfulness"* (Proverbs 14:22). For strangers, this might look like donating $5.00 toward the meal of the person behind you in a fast food drive-thru or paying for the person behind you in line at the coffee shop. You can ask the cashier at the drive-thru to tell the per-son behind you that God prompted you to pay for them because He loves them. (Don't forget to tell the cashier he or she is loved as well.) If you are standing in line at a coffee shop or other restaurant, you can personally tell the person that you want to donate to their purchase, and then ask them if they need prayer for anything, or share with them any words from the Father's heart you are sensing.

In your neighborhood you could clean people's car windows (after checking with them so you don't set off car alarms) and tell them God prompted you to love them for Him. Or you could bake cookies, rake leaves or pull their trash bin in for them on trash day. When possible, share words of knowledge, encouraging prophecy or whatever your faith level is ready to share. If you're available and willing, the Holy Spirit will lead you.

When you're struggling to love family members, ask the Holy Spirit to give you creative ideas for showing them love in tangible ways. It could be words of affirmation and kindness, scratching or massaging their back, doing their chores, buying a small gift, writing a sweet note or doing any number of acts of love.

In the midst of challenges with our youngest daughter, the Holy Spirit prompted me to wash her feet and rub them with lotion every night. She was probably fourteen at the time. As I massaged her feet, I affirmed her and prayed for her out loud. I did this for about six weeks. I didn't see evidence that it changed her heart long-term, but it did soften mine.

I told my children while they were growing up, "You often have to do love before you feel love." This is true with family, friends, neighbors and strangers. Love will grow as you do the *do*. *Do everything in love"* (1 Corinthians 16:14).

Again, don't become stressed by all the good things you want to do for people. You are only one person, so simply live moment by moment in the Lord's presence and He will guide you.

Shyness is Not of God

If you have been falling in love with Jesus and praying for people wherever you go, but you're still too afraid to share God's love because of your shyness, then you need to realize shyness is not of God. I speak from experience because I used to be extremely shy with strangers. The Holy Spirit showed me that my shyness and fear were a result of my pride. I was more concerned about saying something stupid and looking foolish than I was about honoring the people I was around by engaging them in a simple, friendly conversation. It's great to be a quieter person and more of a listener than a talker, but people need to be loved through your words— general questions of interest and words of kindness—as well as words from the Lord.

No matter your age or the age difference of the people you are with, it's important to express love and concern with your words. I was recently around a young man who was very shy. I had to carry the conversation every time we spoke by coming up with questions to ask him because he never asked me any questions about my day or about me. I'm sure he didn't realize it, but the message he sent was that he didn't care about me as a person. Having been in his place, I realized his fear of saying the wrong thing was keeping him from saying anything at all.

FREEDOM FROM SHYNESS

Recognizing and turning from pride and fear is the first step to freedom from shyness. The second step is breaking off the lies of the enemy telling you that people don't want to hear what you have to say or that you'll embarrass yourself if you do talk. The third step is realizing the truth and knowing who you are in Christ. What you have to say is of great value because God made you unique and special. No one in the world is like you and looks at the world exactly like you do. If that's not enough to convince you, the fact that you have God living inside you makes your words even more of a treasure. And finally, force yourself to speak. Focus on questions you can ask people about themselves and then go from there.

In summary, the steps to freedom from shyness are:

- Recognize your pride and fear, and turn from them
- Break off the lies of the devil causing you to be insecure
- Learn your great value to God and the world
- Force yourself to speak—ask people questions and start conversations

PRACTICE INTERACTING

If you've been too shy or uninterested in interacting with people, then begin practicing. Make a list of questions you can ask people in different settings. My mother and I did this when I returned from my first summer with Teen Missions International as a thirteen year old. I had been so shy that my first two weeks of the trip were lonely and miserable until I began making friends and opening up. When I went on my second summer-long trip with Teen Missions the following year, I asked questions from my list, and I developed friendships with all forty team members from the start. It was a blast, and I made a lot of teammates feel good as I showed interest in them. At that age, I asked questions like how old are you? Where are you from? Do you like sports, music, art or other activities? Asking about their interests would often open up the conversation because most people enjoy talking about what excites them.

The questions will vary with the age and the setting, but the key point is that people want to know, and need to know, they're important. I remember as a young child and a teenager being ignored or barely acknowledged by many adults, and what a difference it made when an adult acted interested in me. As a teenager, I decided I would do my best to make children and teenagers feel included and special no matter how old I got, and I hope I'm living up to that goal.

Another great way to practice interacting is to compliment people. We females especially like to be complimented on something we are wearing or how nice we look. If you're a guy, you need to be appropriate and not come across flirtatious, but other females have more freedom in this area. A kind word about a lady's dress or hairstyle may be the only kind word she's received in months.

In a work or school setting, you can compliment people's character (kindness, integrity or work ethic) or their accomplishments (projects or talents), so you have more to work with when praying about what to say.

Proverbs 16:24 says, *"Pleasant words are a honeycomb, sweet to the soul and healing to the bones."* Science has proven that pleasant words literally do bring healing to people's bodies, so make it your goal to bring healing wherever you go.

As you practice interacting with cashiers, waiters, people standing in line with you or other kids at school, your heart will continue to expand and your love will grow. They will become real people rather than just part of a faceless crowd. You'll love them too much *not* to share words and gifts from God's heart.

Expressions of God's Love

If you're still growing in your faith and are not quite ready to step out and speak as if you are speaking the very words of God with prophecy, words of knowledge and words of wisdom, then start by simply expressing God's love.

God loves everyone passionately, so ask the Holy Spirit to highlight people whom He wants to love through you. When He highlights someone, they'll stand out to you and you'll feel a desire to talk with them. At this point in my journey, when someone stands out to me, a sense of God's tremendous love for that person usually floods my mind and heart. That happened a few hours ago.

⊱God's Love Brings Joy⊰

Richelle and cute little Ryder (who is currently twenty months old) had visited and were leaving when I noticed a lady walking on the other side of the street. After I said good-bye to Richelle and Ryder, I grabbed the mail from the mailbox, but I was feeling a flood of God's love for this middle-aged lady who was now several houses down. I almost said *no* to the prompting because she was getting further away from me, but I resisted the devil's attempts to talk me out of it, and I began jogging toward her.

When I was close enough I called out to her, "Ma'am. Excuse me." She stopped and looked at me. "I noticed you when you were down by my house."

"Did I drop something?" she asked.

"No," I said as I crossed the street and joined her on the sidewalk. "I felt a strong sense of God's love for you, so I wanted to tell you how much you mean to Him." Tears immediately sprang to her eyes and began flowing down her cheeks. "I feel like you are dealing with challenges—maybe with a child." Her tears increased, but she was too choked up to speak. I gently put my hand on her shoulder. "Is there something I can pray with you about?"

"My daughter was paralyzed nine years ago so I quit my job to take care of her...." This precious lady, Nelda, opened up and shared the ache in her heart for her grown daughter, the challenges of finding reliable help and some of the other frustrations overwhelming her. Nelda and I talked and prayed together there on the sidewalk for about ten minutes until she got a phone call and had to leave. She put my name and cell phone number in her phone and we hugged each other good-bye. "Thank you so much!" she said.

"Call or stop by anytime. I live right over there," I said as I pointed to our house.

A little later I received a text from her. She said, "Hi, Julie! I'm still in awe over you being bold for God, and speaking to me and praying with me! Thank you for that! I'll remember it forever!"

We sent several texts back and forth. In a later text she wrote, "Thanks again for my blessing! I told everyone about it on Face-book!! People need to know and hear God still works like this!! I probably cried for an hour of joy!"

Even if I hadn't sensed that word of knowledge about her child, the Holy Spirit would have still ministered His tender love to her heart when I expressed God's love for her. So if you aren't yet sure about listening for God's voice, listen for God's love and start there.

Ask God to express His heart of love through you. Express God's delight, concern, vision and forgiveness.

God's delight: You were created in God's image (Genesis 1:27) and you are the apple of His eye (Psalm 17:8). His thoughts toward you outnumber the sand in the sea (Psalm 139:17-18).

God's concern: God counts the hairs on your head (Luke 12:7). He keeps your tears in a bottle (Psalm 56:8 NKJV). He has given you everything you need for life and godliness (2 Peter 1:3).

God's vision: God has incredible plans for your life (Jeremiah 29:11). You can do everything through Christ who strengthens you (Philippians 4:13). You are more than a conqueror through Him who loves you (Romans 8:37).

God's forgiveness: God's greatest act of love was allowing Jesus to die for your sins (Isaiah 53:5). When you make Jesus the Lord [in charge] of your life and believe that God raised Him from the dead, you will be saved from the consequences of your sin and able to spend now and eternity in God's presence (Romans 10:9-10).

You don't need to quote these verses or word it like I did, but the point is people need to know these truths. Even one of these truths can change their life. They need to know they are loved beyond measure, and that no matter how far they run or how many bad things they do, nothing *"will be able to separate us from the love of God that is in Christ Jesus our Lord"* (Romans 8:38-39).

God will love them for eternity—even if He doesn't get to spend eternity with them. Even if a person doesn't humble their heart, admit they need Jesus' forgiveness, and believe that Jesus is Lord—God will still love them. *"I have loved you with an everlasting love"* (Jeremiah 31:3). Once they die, they will be outside the influence of God's love, and no longer able to experience His love, but that doesn't mean God will stop *feeling* intense love for them.

Understanding this concept helps us understand the passage in 2 Timothy 2:11-13:

Here is a trustworthy saying: If we died with Him, we will also live with Him; if we endure, we will also reign with Him. If we disown Him, He will also disown us; if we are faithless, He will remain faithful, for He cannot disown Himself.

If a person disowns God, rejecting God's offer to be His child through Jesus' forgiveness, then God will disown that person. They won't be His child and won't spend eternity with Him.

But...even if that person disowns God and has no faith in who God says He is, and they are completely faithless, God will still be faithful to love them for eternity—because LOVE is who God is. He can't disown Himself because He can't disown love. Even if someone is completely devoid of faith and trust in God, God will remain faithful to love them forever.

I can't begin to imagine the intensity of such love.

I always thought God's love for people in hell would cease once they were outside the influence of His love. But, no, His love is truly everlasting.

With such unfathomable love for each of us, can you imagine the depth of God's pain when even one person rejects Him and His offer to be saved from the penalty of sin? When even one person spends eternity without Him in *"the eternal fire prepared for the devil and his angels"?* (Matthew 25:41).

The magnitude of God's love is hitting me as never before, and I can't stop weeping. I've been weeping for over an hour. A heart-wrenching, deep cry from my spirit that won't stop.

I'm weeping for those who reject God and will spend their lives and eternity without Him....

I'm weeping for God's indescribable pain in losing even one of His beloved creation....

I'm weeping for the body of Christ because we must wake up and express God's incredible love and truth to our world.

How Much Do You Love?

Given the intensity of God's never-ending love for every individual, please ask yourself, *How much do I truly love God and care about His heart? Do I care that His heart will ache for eternity over each person who rejects Him?*

How much do I truly love people? Do I care that without Jesus' forgiveness they will spend eternity in hell in eternal torment apart from any influence or effect of God's love?

I'm positive you care deeply because you're reading this book.

Jesus said, *"If anyone would come after me, he must deny himself and take up his cross and follow me"* (Matthew 16:24). Because God's power is in you, you can choose to:

- Love people no matter the cost.
- Listen expectantly to the Holy Spirit.
- Say *yes* and share God's words and love gifts.

When you get to heaven, you will be among the group of whom

God will say: *"They overcame him* [the devil] *by the blood of the Lamb and by the word of their testimony; they did not love their lives so much as to shrink from death"* (Revelation 12:11). God will say, *"Well done— you said YES!"*

When I Didn't Love Enough

Although my goal is to say *yes* to each of the Holy Spirit's prompt-ings, I still have doubts or fears and sometimes I say *no*. Two of those acts of disobedience ended tragically as far as I know, so I want to share them with you.

ROBIN WILLIAMS

I had the strong thought several years ago to send Robin Williams a letter expressing my appreciation for his humor, but most im-portantly to express the Father's love for him. I had only seen the clean movies he acted in, but he had made me laugh, and I love to laugh. We don't have TV and only watch DVDs and videos, so I knew very little about him personally, but I was pretty sure he wasn't a believer. It seemed impossible to reach someone as famous as Robin, so I figured this was a silly thought and I ignored it.

A few months ago the thought popped into my head again. *I wouldn't have the faintest idea how to contact a celebrity*, I thought, and again I dismissed it as just being a crazy notion of mine.

You can imagine how my heart sank when I was checking my Facebook posts on August 11, 2014, just two months later, and read the news: Robin Williams was dead. He was not only dead, but he had committed suicide.

I didn't have a clue that Robin had issues with depression, but God knew. Knowing Robin's battle with despair and hopelessness, the Father had asked me to express His great love for Robin and the hope we have in Jesus…but I ignored His promptings.

I laid my head on my desk and wept.

Oh, Father, I am so sorry. I didn't trust Your still small voice speaking to my thoughts. What would it have cost me to have at least attempted to write him? Only a stamp and a little time. I know You have been reaching out to him with Your love his whole life, but You asked me to reach out yet another time, and I didn't do it.

I searched the Internet hoping to find an article saying that Robin had found Christ's love and forgiveness before he died, but I couldn't find one. I hope Robin did cry out to Jesus in his last moments on the earth, but I won't know until I get to heaven and look for him. As far as I can tell, his story ended tragically and he is spending eternity without the God who loved him beyond comprehension.

A GRANDMA AND GRANDPA

I had a similar story about seven years ago. Richelle became friends with a young woman at a new church we were attending. The friend was telling us one day about how poorly her grandparents were doing physically, and she asked us to pray for them. When I asked if they were Christians, she said she didn't think so.

The following week she told us they were getting worse. The strong thought sprang to my mind to drive to see them and express God's love and forgiveness. They lived several states away, so it would have been at least a fifteen hour drive. The thought hung with me, but the devil shot his lies and doubts at me—and I believed him. *Who am I that they would even listen to me? Where would I stay and how could I squeeze this expense into the budget? Surely this is just me and not God's prompting.* I prayed for her grandparents when they came to mind, but I dismissed the idea of driving to see them.

We didn't see this friend for several months since the church has several services each Sunday. When we did see her again, I asked about her grandparents. "They died," she said. When she told me more details, I realized her grandmother died two weeks after I had been prompted to go talk with them. Her grandfather had then died less than two weeks after his wife. The family wasn't sure they ever gave their hearts to the Lord.

Accountable

I was stunned and grieved, and I told the Lord I would never do that again. But here I was dealing with this same grief with Robin Williams. Ezekiel 33:8 came to mind: *"When I say to the wicked, 'O wicked man, you will surely die,' and you do not speak out to dissuade him from his ways, that wicked man will die for his sin, and I will hold you accountable for his blood."*

I am under the blood of Jesus and all of my sins are forgiven, unlike in Old Testament times before Jesus came, but I believe I am still accountable for the words God gives me to share and the actions He tells me to take. I don't believe I'll be punished for all the things I didn't do because that punishment was taken by Jesus, but I do have to live with the knowledge that I might have been one of the last Christians God tried to use one more time to reach Robin Williams and those two precious grandparents before it was too late. I don't live under condemnation, but I do live under increased conviction that I must listen and do my part.

I discovered what appears to be the heartbreaking ending to their stories, but think about all the endings we will never hear about until we get to heaven. Think about all the people we ignored because we weren't listening or we weren't willing to say *yes*. God is constantly working in people's lives, but He has chosen to use us to express His love and to share the good news that Jesus is Lord. They won't hear if we don't tell them. *"And how can they believe in the one of whom they have not heard? And how can they hear without someone preaching to them?"* (Romans 10:14). You and I must love people enough to say *yes* to God's promptings.

Chapter Highlights and Application

Begin Praying Silently for People Everywhere You Go: This simple act of praying for people wherever you go will radically transform your life. As you pray blessings over people, your love *for* them will overcome your fear *of* them. You will become a fearless warrior of love whose only concern is to love God and love people by living in radical obedience to God's voice. So go for it! Begin praying silently for people when you're driving, at work, at school, at the grocery store and at the gym. Then watch in amazement as God changes your heart, frees you from fear and fills you with love.

Practice Interacting with People: Love people with words of kindness and encouragement. You can comment on behaviors, good attitudes, someone's smile, something they are wearing, how nice they look and on and on. This blesses the person while it helps you overcome your fear of talking with people. Even talking about the weather is better than not talking at all. But don't stop there. People need to know they are on God's heart.

Express God's Heart of Love and Delight: You have the privilege of expressing God's heart of love and delight for people. Share with people that God is passionately in love with them, and then trust God to give you specific words of love, words of knowledge and words of prophecy about the amazing things God has in store for them. Love people enough to simply tell them the good news—they are loved beyond measure and Jesus made a way for them to be saved from their sin and saved from an eternity without God!

Chapter 12

Know Who You Are and Whose You Are

"Who's that superhero transforming our city?"

"It's the Parcel Wonder making deliveries for God's Parcel Service!" shouted a teenager from the crowd.

An elderly woman spoke up. "I felt all alone after my husband died, but the Parcel Wonder approached me at the grocery store and delivered words of comfort and love directly from the Father's heart to remind me I'm never alone."

"I was debating whether to start my own business," said a college student, "when the Parcel Wonder delivered a word to me at the coffee shop that the business I had in mind was from God and to go ahead with the schooling I needed to make it happen."

A young mother spoke with tears in her eyes, "I was visiting with a friend outside a restaurant when the Parcel Wonder sat down with us and shared words of love from God's heart, and then led us to receive Jesus' forgiveness. Now my family is walking with God!"

"I had strayed from God and was hurting," said another young woman, "when the Parcel Wonder was prompted to stop and talk with me in front of CVS late one night, and I recommitted my heart to Jesus. I still struggle to keep my eyes on Him, but I've never forgotten that night."

"I was homeless and my foot was in terrible pain when the Parcel Wonder delivered a gift of healing and all the pain instantly left," said a middle-aged woman.

"I was homeless," said a woman in her sixties, "when the Parcel Wonder was prompted to give me a ride, and shortly after that was prompted to bring me home. I was told I was the Father's princess."

A fireman piped in, "I had just gone through a painful divorce when the Parcel Wonder was prompted to stop at our fire station to deliver a message to someone who had been through a divorce or a death in the family. The Parcel Wonder wrote me a note telling me God cares for me and loves me…and I'm not alone."

Yes, these are my stories, but the Parcel Wonder isn't just me.

The Parcel Wonder is you.

The Parcel Wonder is every Christian who says *yes* to God.

As soon as you believe in Jesus and invite the Holy Spirit to baptize you in His love and power, you become a superhero and a Parcel Wonder. The power of God dwells in you, and you have the same power that raised Christ from the dead (see Romans 8:11). You have the power to not only speak God's words, but to heal the sick, raise the dead, cast out demons and even tell mountains and the weather what to do! All these gifts, these parcels, are in your truck and ready to be delivered.

If this is true, then why are most of us (myself included) not see-ing all these things happen? It isn't because the gifts have ceased, because Jesus told the apostles in Matthew 28:19-20 to go and make disciples of all nations and teach them to obey *everything* He com-manded them. Jesus clearly commanded them to *"Heal the sick, raise the dead, cleanse those who have leprosy, drive out demons. Freely you have received, freely give"* (Matthew 10:8). This means that every Christian in every nation is supposed to obey this command, too. Many people around the world are seeing God move in the miracu-lous, but what about those of us who aren't? Why aren't we seeing more of God's power?

The reason we aren't is because we haven't fully powered up our Super Suits.

Your Super Suit

From the moment you become a believer you are clothed in a Super Suit. This Super Suit not only gives you the ability to teach, prophesy, heal the sick, drive out demons and raise the dead, but it gives you the ability to love, forgive and walk in holiness.

What is this Super Suit made of? Well, the better question would be *who* is this Super Suit made of? *"You are all sons of God through faith in Christ Jesus, for all of you who were baptized into Christ have clothed yourselves with Christ"* (Galatians 3:26-27).

Your Super Suit is made of Jesus!

"On that day you will realize that I am in my Father, and you are in Me, and I am in you" (John 14:20). Jesus is not only in you, but you are in Him. You are literally clothed with Jesus. That is why Paul goes on to say in Galatians 3:28, *"There is neither Jew nor Greek, slave nor free, male nor female, for you are all one in Christ Jesus."* When the Father looks at you He doesn't see your nationality, your social status or your gender. He sees Jesus.

You are in Christ Jesus—totally forgiven, totally loved and totally empowered!

POWERING UP

The devil knows the power that resides in you and on you through Jesus, so his demons constantly spew lies to keep you from powering up. They tell you:

Power is no longer available to Christians.

God isn't healing, doing miracles or speaking.

The Bible is all you need.

God wants you sick to teach you lessons.

You are unworthy.

You can't hear God.

You have to earn God's power.

God doesn't care.

God is angry.

And on and on….

The devil's goal is to distort your view of yourself and your view of God so that he can rob you of your identity and confidence. If he can keep you from knowing who you are and whose you are, he can keep you powerless.

Who Are You?

Early in the summer of 2014 I was talking with Jesus while I washed dishes. "If You were born as a baby like I was, and if You had to grow in wisdom like I do, and if You had all the same limitations and challenges I have, then why were You able to do all those miracles and I'm not?"

Jesus responded lovingly and passionately: *"Because I knew who I was."*

Tears welled up in my eyes. I understood the concept of knowing my identity in Christ, but the intensity of His words shook me. As I pondered what He said, a resolve rose up in my spirit. "That's it! I need to do whatever it takes to better understand and truly absorb into my heart who I am and the authority God has given me!" In the past, when I read good books or listened to great teachings by people who were experiencing breakthrough in seeing the power of God, I would get fired up for a while, but when I didn't see results in my own life, especially in the area of healing, I'd get distracted by other things and quit pushing forward.

I realized that if I'm going to be like Jesus and see people saved, healed and set free, then I shouldn't give up until the devil's lies are replaced with God's truth in my mind and soul. I need to "hang out" with people who are seeing more of God's power because they have a better grasp of who they are and who God is. I need to figure out what they believe that I have yet to discover.

ANDREW WOMMACK AND DUANE SHERIFF

I had heard that a man named Andrew Wommack[16] had seen a lot of breakthrough in healing, so I looked him up on the Internet a few days later. I watched the testimonies on his website of people who had grasped what Andrew was saying about God's desire to heal everyone, and our authority over illness, and how they were then able to receive healing for themselves and for others. They were discovering who God was and who they were in Christ, and the result was a faith that was moving their mountains.

Just for grins, I thought I'd look up Andrew Wommack's schedule to see if there was any chance he was speaking nearby sometime soon. Isn't it just like God that Andrew was speaking on-ly an hour away at Victory Life Church in Durant, Oklahoma in less than two weeks.

I not only went to the conference, but God put me smack dab behind Andrew during one of the sessions when another speaker was sharing. After the session, I tapped Andrew on the shoulder and asked him several questions about things I was still grappling with in regard to healing, and he graciously answered my ques-tions. He and his wife prayed with me for breakthrough in my own faith.

While at the conference, I discovered the pastor of Victory Life Church, Duane Sheriff[17], has also walked in healing and health for many years and has a passion for people to understand their identi-ty in Christ. He gives away his incredible teaching CDs at no charge because he wants people to be free from the lies of the enemy and full of faith for the miraculous.

I loaded up on Duane's healing CDs and bought three of An-drew's books: *The Believer's Authority*, *God Wants You Well* and *The True Nature of God*. I've sat under many incredible teachers and I study the Bible extensively, but these teachings not only confirmed what the Holy Spirit had already shown me in many areas, but they brought tremendous and exciting clarity in regard to God's view on healing and our authority on the earth.

If you are hungry to understand your authority and to do the works of Jesus, I encourage you to look up their websites below and order these three books by Andrew Wommack and the free CDs by Duane Sheriff. They have numerous books and teachings, but this will give you a place to start.

Andrew Wommack's website: www.awmi.net:

The Believer's Authority (book)

God Wants You Well (book)

The True Nature of God (book)

Duane Sheriff's website: www.dsheriff.org:

God's Sovereignty, Man's Authority (CD set)

Healing I and II (2 CD sets)

Training for Reigning (CD set)

Andrew Wommack, Duane Sheriff and many others have come to understand their authority over sickness, disease and every attack of the enemy, and they are seeing the fruit of their faith. Andrew Wommack's son was dead for five hours before Andrew found out he was dead. He and his wife began praying from where they were, and five minutes later their son came back to life and sat up in the hospital morgue—with no brain damage. Now that's knowing your authority!

Completely Forgiven

Realizing how God sees you in relation to sin is crucial to powering up your Super Suit. If you believe the devil's lies that you're a wretch barely saved by grace who has to constantly grovel before the Lord, then you'll rarely feel worthy enough to get out of your delivery truck, let alone have faith to believe God wants to show His power through you.

God no longer sees your sin because you are forgiven and you are in Christ. *"Therefore, there is now no condemnation for those who are in Christ Jesus"* (Romans 8:1). Andrew Wommack does a fantastic job explaining this in his book, *The True Nature of God.* Please read slowly as I quote portions of Chapter 4. He uses the King James Version.

> *"Therefore if any man be in Christ, he is a new creature: old things are passed away; behold, all things are become new. And all things are of God, who hath reconciled us to Himself by Jesus Christ"* (2 Corinthians 5:17-18).

When you were saved, you became a new creature. Your spirit on the inside was changed….Your body and all your physical features didn't change and become different. Your mind didn't change. *Your spirit is the part of you that was changed.*

"A new heart also will I give you, and a new spirit will I put within you: and I will take away the stony heart out of your flesh, and I will give you an heart of flesh" (Ezekiel 36:26).

We are new spirits who are righteous and holy. There is no sin in our spirits. Jesus became sin for us so that we might be *made* the righteousness of God. We did not get a little bit of the righteousness of God just to get us through life. We have the *total* righteousness of God in our spirits. Our spirits are as complete and perfect within us right this moment as they will ever be throughout all eternity.

"Herein is our love made perfect, that we may have boldness in the day of judgment: because as he is, so are we in this world" (1 John 4:17).

"As He is, so are we in this world." It is not "so are we going to be," but so are we *now*....And this verse is saying our spirits are ounce-for-ounce and molecule-for-molecule (if there are such things in the spiritual realm) identical to the Lord Jesus Christ's spirit! Our spirits are totally His workmanship. They're clean and pure. And if we sin, our spirits are never contaminated because it's not our spirits that sin.

"Whosoever is born of God doth not commit sin; for his seed remaineth in him; and he cannot sin, because he is born of God" (1 John 3:9).

The spirit is the only part of us that is born of God — and it cannot sin. It does not sin. It's the seed of God within us. We've never sinned with our spirit man. We're enticed in the realm of the flesh, and our emotions and our minds may get into sin because our will chooses it. But our spirits are not participating in sin.

When I come before God and say "Abba, Father," God isn't looking at my sins and the ways I've fallen short. He isn't seeing those things and saying, "How dare you come before Me in your sin!" That's because I didn't come before Him in my sin—I came before Him in my perfect, sinless spirit and in truth!

God looks at my spirit. No matter what my flesh has done, my spirit is pure, holy, complete, spotless, and undefiled. God can look at me and have fellowship with me just exactly the same as He would with the Lord Jesus Christ!

Now, even though my spirit is pure, my soul and body aren't pure yet. That is the only thing that hinders my fellowship with God. And if I'm wallowing in sin, I'm going to defile my conscience and have a hard time walking in spiritual truth.

The Bible says in 1 Corinthians 2:14 that the natural man cannot receive the things of the spirit. If I'm constantly living in sin in the natural realm, I'm not going to feel like my spirit is pure. God still looks at my spirit and it is just as pure as it ever was, but I'm not going to be able to perceive its purity, because I'm carnally minded. I won't be able to perceive and walk in the spirit realm, experiencing who I am in Christ Jesus. I am locked into the physical realm if I live in sin. Soon I start believing, *God, how could You love me the way I am?*

I believe because our spirits are perfect, they don't have to grow, but growth must take place in our souls. Spiritual truths are already reality and complete in our spirits, but our minds, emotions, and will need to learn and begin to practice them. The Bible calls this partaking of the divine nature, or becoming like God, thinking, speaking, and acting the way He does.

*"Whereby are given unto us exceeding great and precious promis-
es: that by these ye might be partakers of the divine nature, having
escaped the corruption that is in the world through lust"* (2 Peter
1:4).

Simply put, as we renew our minds to God's Word, spend
time in His presence, and form intimate relationship with
Him, the purity and perfection in our spirits will begin to
transform our souls. And when our souls begin to line up
with our spirits, our flesh loses its power to get us to sin.
Our flesh becomes subject to our souls, which have become
subject to our spirits. Therefore, we overcome sin because
we are acting like Jesus.

This is a great picture of being new creatures in Christ, but
what happens if we mess up one day? Instead of saying
"I'm not worthy of You because I blew it," we'll say, "God,
through Jesus' blood, I run back into Your arms and thank
You for forgiving me and cleansing me from all unright-
eousness."

*"For ye have not received the spirit of bondage again to fear; but ye
have received the Spirit of adoption, whereby we cry, Abba, Father"* (Romans 8:15).

—Andrew Wommack, "God's Gift of Eternal Life" in
The True Nature of God, 58-64. Colorado Springs, 2010.

God doesn't see you through your sin. He sees you through
your spirit, and your spirit has been born again and can't sin! You
can have the same fellowship with the Father that Jesus has because
you are completely undefiled in Jesus. This fact always makes me
want to dance, laugh and swing around in the Father's arms.

This truth frees us from the bondage of legalism. Legalism fo-
cuses on our sin and tells us to work harder to change. But God
says we are forgiven, accepted and loved—and out of that love relationship, with our focus on Him, changes automatically begin to
take place. It's a process, but one that's free from guilt and condemnation!

Completely Loved and Empowered

As a believer who is in God's lap, it's vital you understand that God sees you as holy and dearly loved because your perception affects your behavior. If you walk into a party where you feel everyone likes you and thinks you're important, then you'll probably act likable and confident. If you walk into a party where you feel everyone dislikes you or is uninterested in you, then you'll probably act grumpy or hide in the corner.

Your actions reflect your thoughts. If you see yourself as a defeated Christian always struggling with sin, then you'll behave like a defeated Christian always struggling with sin. But if you see yourself as God sees you—righteous, holy and loved—then you will behave like the righteous, holy and loved person you are.

As a child in school I was an average student, but I never felt especially smart. In 4th or 5th grade they gave us some sort of aptitude test and I scored higher than average. When the test told me I was smarter than I thought, I began thinking of myself as a smarter student. As a result of my added confidence, I began making better grades. My ability hadn't changed, but my perception had. It was my perception that changed my behavior.

When you know deep in your heart that you are the righteousness of God in Christ; that God sees you as He sees Jesus; and that you are completely loved beyond anything you can imagine, you will boldly come to the Father as that righteous and loved child.

As you grow in your understanding of your status, authority, privilege, position and power as an honored and beloved child of the King of Kings, your confidence in God's love and your confidence in who you are will explode like fireworks in your spirit—and that explosion of faith is what powers up your Super Suit.

You'll jump out of your GPS truck and be the Parcel Wonder—the superhero—God has empowered you to be. You will look and act like Jesus to your world because you are literally *in Him*. Fear will be replaced with confidence because it's not your power and love you're counting on—it's His!

Who is Our Enemy?

Our enemy, the devil, is the father of lies and he doesn't want you to climb up in Father God's lap and experience a relationship with God that will transform your world and lead many people to Jesus. The devil wants you to stay at a distance and either ignore, fear, hate or at least misunderstand God. He wants you to be ignorant of God's true character of love, and ignorant of the authority you have been given on the earth. With these two misconceptions, Satan can keep you from intimacy with God and from the faith to fully power up your Super Suit.

DISTORTER OF GOD

The devil loves to blame all the anger, violence, sickness, disease, plagues and disasters on God. He loves to tell believers and non-believers that God is in control so everything must be God's fault. Jesus clearly refuted that in John 10:10 (NASB) when He said, *"The thief* [Satan] *comes only to steal and kill and destroy; I came that they may have life, and have it abundantly."* This is a huge topic that Andrew Wommack discusses in his book *The Believer's Authority*. I know it's not normal for an author to so extensively quote another author as I have, but now that you've almost finished reading *No More No*, Andrew and Duane's books and teachings will take you to the next level in walking in power and authority.

Who Has Dominion and Authority?

This is taken from Chapter 6 of Andrew Wommack's book, *The Believer's Authority*, with scriptures from the King James Version:

> The Lord made Adam and Eve the gods of this world.
> *"I have said, Ye are gods; and all of you are children of the most High"* (Psalm 82:6).
> In context, this was God creating man and saying to him, "You are gods." This isn't "Gods" in the sense of divinity, but "gods" in the sense of rulership. We were given dominion—power and authority—over the earth. Since it was ours to rule and reign, we were gods over the earth.

"The heaven, even the heavens, are the LORD's: but the earth hath He given to the children of men" (Psalm 115:16).

God literally gave the earth to mankind. The Creator gave us the power and authority to rule over this earth as if we were the creator. We weren't the Creator, but that's how much dominion He gave us.

I believe that when Lucifer—still the sinless, perfect angel of God in the garden sent to minister to Adam and Eve—saw the unconditional authority over the earth that God had given to man, he recognized an opportunity. Isaiah 14 reveals his thought process.

"O Lucifer, son of the morning...thou hast said in thine heart, I will ascend into heaven, I will exalt my throne above the stars of God: I will sit also upon the mount of the congregation, in the sides of the north: I will ascend above the heights of the clouds: I will be like the most High" (Isaiah 14:12-14).

Lucifer envied God. He wasn't content with being the top angel. He was jealous and wanted God's position, but he couldn't just take that place with the delegated power he had been given. If he would have rebelled, that power would have instantly been taken away and he would have been destroyed. [Andrew explained earlier that this was his supposition.] However, he saw an opportunity with man because God had given Adam and Eve something that He'd never given the angels—an unconditional, no reservations or qualifications, no strings attached authority over the earth. Lucifer saw that if he could get Adam and Eve to yield to him and rebel against God, then he could become the new "god" of this world (see 2 Corinthians 4:4).

"Know you not, that to whom ye yield yourselves servants to obey, his servants ye are to whom ye obey; whether of sin unto death, or of obedience unto righteousness?" (Romans 6:16).

212

Understanding how God's kingdom works, Lucifer knew that if he could trick Adam and Eve into yielding to and obeying him, then he could become their master. Then he could take the power and authority that had been given to mankind and use it to begin thwarting the kingdom of God and start receiving the praise, adoration, and glory that he desired.

As Creator and owner, God could have come down and wiped out the world. He could have destroyed Adam and Eve, the devil, and all of the angels that rebelled. As Creator, He had the right to do that and start over. Yet, to intervene in the affairs of this world like that would have violated His Word. He had given the dominion over this earth to Adam and Eve. He had given the power and authority to rule over this world to physical human beings.

For God to maintain His integrity and stand by what He had previously said—"You have dominion"—He had to give Adam and Eve their freedom. If they wanted to yield their authority and power over the earth to Satan, then technically it was their right to do so.

So we see that Satan is the god of this world because we gave him our dominion and authority when we submitted to him in the Garden of Eden. That's why there is such heartache and grief on the earth. But the good news is that we can take back that authority from Satan. Let's look further at what Andrew says:

Taking Back Our Power and Authority
Many Christians see Satan as an angelic being with godlike supernatural power and authority over man. They see him coming and overpowering them, when the truth is that the devil can't force them to do anything. He lost his power when he rebelled at God. The only power and authority Satan is functioning under now is human power and authority.

It takes your cooperation for the devil to do anything in your life. That's why he seeks whom he *may* devour. Satan doesn't have the authority and power to devour you unless you quit obeying God and yield yourself to sin. Romans 6:16 says that when you yield yourself to sin, you're actually yielding yourself to the author of that sin, which is Satan. Satan can't just come in and destroy you without your cooperation. But when you sin, you are empowering the devil.

Satan can't do anything without somebody in an earthsuit yielding to him. This is why he's constantly vying for your heart, trying to get you to yield to him through anger, fear, hurt, pain, and depression. Every time you move away from what God's Word says and act in union with what the devil is trying to do, you yield authority to him. Every time you quit believing and receiving God's supernatural power and ability and sin instead, you empower the enemy. Satan can only function as he keeps people submitted to himself through lies and deception.

> —Andrew Wommack, "God of This World" in *The Believer's Authority*, 45-52. Tulsa: Harrison House, 2009.

We take back our power and authority by no longer agreeing with the lies of the enemy. These lies could be telling us it's okay to get angry, hold unforgiveness, lie, cheat or sin sexually. These lies could be telling us we aren't worthy of God's love, God can't speak to us clearly or we don't have authority over sickness, disease, death and every evil attack from the devil. We resist the devil by not believing and not acting on his lies. We take back our authority by walking in God's truth and love, and living by faith in every area of our lives.

Can God Lie?

God is incapable of anything but truth.

- If God says you are loved—you are loved immeasurably.

- If God says you are righteous—you are holy in His sight.
- If God says His sheep hear His voice—you can hear Him clearly.
- If God says go into all the world and preach—you are equipped to share wherever you go.
- If God says you have been given the gifts of the Spirit— you are supernaturally empowered.

So when you are at the grocery, work, school or the coffee shop, ask yourself: Does God lie?

Then answer yourself: No. He is incapable of lying. It is an impossibility. Everything He says is absolute truth. That means I can do everything He commanded me to do. I can walk in victory over sin, lead people to Jesus, share words of prophecy and love, see sick people healed, take authority over the weather and command demons to flee. I can do everything Jesus did—and more.

The only thing able to stop you is your lack of faith. You must trust God and His words, and step out by faith to share His love gifts with your world wherever you go. God is your all-powerful, all-knowing Father and you are His beloved, called and empowered child. *"I can do all things through Christ who strengthens me"* (Philippians 4:13 NKJV). You have been given power and authority to do God's will on the earth because you are truly a superhero!

Chapter Highlights and Application

You are a Superhero: The reason you probably enjoy superhero stories is because you were created to be a superhero. You were made to operate in supernatural power and love. It's part of who you are. The devil has twisted this desire for power, and caused people to destroy each other through fighting, wars and lies. But this desire for power, when it operates hand-in-hand with God's love, was meant to do tremendous good on the earth. Jesus was our example of what God meant for our lives to look like once we discover who we are and the power and authority we've been given.

I pray you will join with me and never give up until you and I are walking in all the power and love we've been promised. Let's keep breaking free from the devil's lies until we are living like Jesus. Please get a copy of Andrew Wommack's book, *The Believer's Authority,* and the other books and/or audio teachings I mentioned. Satan's stinking lies are all that's stopping us from living in God's truth. *"Then you will know the truth, and the truth will set you free"* (John 8:32). Knowing the truth will set you free from fear, sin, sickness, depression and every attack of the enemy.

See Yourself as God Sees You: You aren't a lowly sinner saved by grace and struggling to walk in victory. You are a righteous and holy child of God and an overcomer. You have the same fellowship with the Father that Jesus has because you are in Christ. You are a new creation and a partaker of the Divine nature. You are no longer sin-stained and walking in guilt and condemnation because all your sins—past, present and future sins—have been cleansed. Live every day in this revelation and watch how your behaviors begin to match the truth, and an amazing transformation will take place in your life.

You Can Do It!

No matter what you're like—quiet or outgoing, laidback or driven, a new believer or mature in Christ—you can say *No More No* and live a *Yes, Lord* lifestyle. You can be the superhero—the Parcel Wonder—God has equipped you to be. It all comes down to three things:

Faith, Hope and Love

❖ **Stepping out by *faith* and taking daily risks**

❖ **Seeing miracles with the eyes of your heart (*hope*)**

❖ **Staying immersed in and expressing God's *love***

When you wake up in the morning tell Jesus:

I love You and I receive Your amazing love for me. I choose to walk in Your love, see Your vision for each situation and step out by faith. You said, *"Everything is possible for him who believes"* (Mark 9:23), so I choose to believe and watch the impossible happen today.

I will open my mouth by faith, trusting You will give me Your words.

I will pray for the sick and oppressed, believing You want them healthy and free.

I will not allow the devil to keep me fearful, full of doubt, silent or passive because there is a world desperate for Your love and power.

I will say *yes* to everything You ask me to do today because I love You and I trust You.

It's important to daily build up your faith. You can build it up through proclamations similar to this one, through immersing yourself in God's Word and through reading, listening to and hanging out with others who are walking in power and love. The devil will constantly attempt to tear down your faith by shooting you with his lies and by using others to attack your faith. Jude 17-19 talks about how scoffers will attack and divide believers because scoffers follow mere natural instincts rather than the Spirit.

As a born-again, Spirit-filled believer, you no longer live according to safe, natural instincts. You live a "super" natural life of faith and risk. Your life is about stepping out on the water, operating in the gifts of the Spirit and being the hands and voice of Jesus wherever you go.

It's important to build up your faith and walk in God's love for you every moment of every day. *"But you, dear friends, build yourselves up in your most holy faith and pray in the Holy Spirit. Keep yourselves in God's love as you wait for the mercy of our Lord Jesus Christ to bring you to eternal life."* (Jude 20-21).

The following two stories of mine are recent examples of the importance of focusing on love and building up our faith:

❧Focused on Love—Not Feelings❧

My doctor and I have been working to balance my hormones and thyroid while I wait for breakthrough in healing. I had been feeling great for several months, but the last three days I could tell my body was getting out of whack as I became increasingly emotional, exhausted and forgetful. I felt groggy and ready to crawl in a hole and hide. I even stopped by the library and picked out a couple Christian fiction books (something I rarely do) so that I could ignore my reality and pretend to be the beautiful, loved heroine of the story.

When I realized I was turning to the wrong source for help, I immediately turned my focus back to loving Jesus and receiving

His love for me. It made an immediate difference in my emotions. I still felt physically yucky, but I was at peace and again enjoying Jesus' presence.

Shortly after that, I stopped by the grocery store. I prayed as I walked in. *Jesus, I love You and I know You love me. I don't have the least bit of energy or desire to talk to anyone, but I'm not going to focus on my feelings. I'm going to focus on Your love. You are delighted in me as Your precious daughter and I am delighted in You....*

I continued basking in His love as I got a cart. As I walked through the inner doors, the Holy Spirit highlighted a man sitting in the restaurant just inside the store. God's love for this man flooded my heart and it no longer mattered how I felt.

"Hi," I said as I pushed my cart near him. "I felt like the Lord wanted me to come and tell you how much you mean to Him. He loves you, and I see Him gathering you in His arms."

"Thank you. That's very kind of you to say." The man appeared to be in his late fifties.

"Do you have much of a relationship with Him yet?"

"Not really. I pray sometimes and I used to go to church as a child, but I haven't been to church in a long time."

"It's not about church anyway. It's about having a relationship with God by asking Jesus to forgive you and live inside you. It's about surrendering your life to Him—to His guidance and wisdom....Sin keeps us from God, but Jesus died so that we could be forgiven and be with Him here on earth and for eternity....God isn't trying to throw people into hell. He's doing everything He can to keep us out of hell and get us to heaven....God made you extremely special and He misses you because He created you to do life with Him."

I went on to share how my mother went from being a religious church goer to becoming a Christian, and how I did the same—and the difference God made in our lives.

"I've heard stories of God really changing people's lives," he said.

"Yes, it's true. When God's Spirit comes to live inside you, you're changed by His love!"

We spoke for about ten minutes before the person he was waiting for called him on is cell phone.

"Thank you for talking with me," he said. "As I've gotten older, I've been thinking more about these things, and I've been thinking I need to go to church."

"Let me give you a hug," I said as he stood. "God's got amazing things in store for you as you begin a relationship with Him!" He gladly returned the hug and had a huge smile on his face when he said good-bye and walked away.

If I hadn't turned my focus from my feelings to Jesus' love for me and my love for Jesus, this man wouldn't have heard these words of truth from Jesus' heart. Staying focused on God's love is essential. Jesus knew the importance of living our lives surrounded in His love. He said in John 15:9: *As the Father has loved me, so have I loved you. Now remain in my love.*"

When Jesus' love—God's love—fills our hearts, there's no room for fear, doubt or selfishness. All that we are concerned with is loving Him and pleasing His heart. Nothing else matters.

❧Building Up My Faith❧

I had just finished writing this book when I had an onslaught of doubts and lies attack my thoughts. "You can't hear God. You'll never see people healed. You don't have enough financial or volunteer support to start this ministry." On and on the attacks continued relentlessly for several weeks. I recognized what was happening and rebuked the enemy and silenced his lies numerous times, but I allowed my confidence to dwindle, so it was getting harder to hear from the Lord for people.

The only way the devil can stop any of us from operating in the supernatural is by weakening our faith, and he had weakened mine substantially.

The next time I was at church I chose to take back my authority and build up my faith during worship. I fell to my knees and raised my arms there at the front of the church, desperate to be free again from the lies.

I rebuked the lies and proclaimed the truth:
I have been filled with the Spirit and He has given me all His gifts

in order to bless my world with words of prophecy, healing, miracles and every good thing in Christ. I can hear God and I will share prophetic words and miracles from His heart wherever I go.

It was an amazing and refreshing time in God's presence.

Later, during the message, I paused to ask the Holy Spirit: *Is there anyone here You want to speak to? Anyone You want to bless? Just show me. I'm willing. I choose to believe and step out by faith, because faith not accompanied by deeds is dead* (see James 2:17).

Ten minutes later, the Holy Spirit impressed on me the lady sitting two seats away. She was here visiting relatives, so I'd never met her before this evening. *Bless her, Holy Spirit, and show me what You want to say or do through me.* I immediately had the thought that she was in the midst of a painful relationship with a man. I wasn't sure if it was her husband or a boyfriend.

When the church service was over, I quickly grabbed her attention. "The Lord highlighted you to me during the service. Are you in the midst of a painful situation with a man?" She didn't have a ring on her left hand so I asked, "Is it with a boyfriend?"

"Yes," she said as her eyes immediately teared up.

"Can I pray with you for healing and wisdom?" I asked gently.

"Yes, please. I'm in the midst of some tough decisions."

As I prayed for her and we continued to talk, the Holy Spirit encouraged her that she will know without a doubt when she meets the man she is to marry. Her husband won't be perfect, but he will love God above all else. The rest of the conversation is private, but it was an honor to pass on God's heart and His words of love for His precious daughter.

⋅⋅⋅❦⋅⋅⋅

I never feel highly prophetic or especially gifted when I step out by faith and choose to be confident. But I step out by faith with confidence because I have a really BIG GOD, and my really BIG GOD promised to speak, work and love through me.

You, too, have a really BIG GOD who has promised to speak, work and love through you. The only thing required to activate that power is for you to step out by faith and go for it—share a word, believe for healing, free the oppressed from demonic attack and command those mountains to move in Jesus' name! *"According to your faith will it be done to you"* (Matthew 9:29).

You can do it!

Please Stay in Touch

Thank you for taking a peek at my world and allowing me to share my heart. If you don't agree with everything I said, that's okay. Please apply what you can and put the rest on the back burner to "taste" it again later and see if it's more palatable at another time.

I would love to hear from you, so please find me on Facebook and visit my website to read more stories and to share your own. I'd love to hear how God is using you to express His love and gifts wherever you go.

I'm praying for each person who reads *No More No,* and you've become very special to me. Hopefully we will meet one day, but if I don't have the privilege of meeting you here on earth, let's definitely attend some parties together in heaven and have a number of long chats. I'd be thrilled and honored!

Many blessings ~ *Julie*

CURRENT ADDRESSES:
www.CrazyAboutYou.org
or www.JulieEarl.com
and
www.Facebook.com/CrazyAboutYouMinistries
https://Twitter.com/JulieEarlCAYM

If you were blessed or encouraged by *No More No,* please share it on Facebook and Twitter, and go to Amazon and write a review and buy a few more books to give away so that others can be inspired to say *yes!*

For personal or group Bible studies done in conjunction with *No More No,* look for the *No More No Bible Study Guide* to be released summer 2015.

Bonus Materials

God's Love for You

First John 4:8 says, "God is love." God doesn't just behave in a loving manner. He *is* love. He is perfect, complete and faultless love, and He loves you perfectly, completely and faultlessly. You can trust that everything He does and says is out of love for you.

If you have not understood and experienced God's incredible love for you, go back and read Chapter 10 "Fall in Love with Jesus" and ask God to open your eyes to see all the ways He has reached out in love to you. The devil has attempted to destroy you with lies, sin, sickness and disease, but God has been blessing you and drawing you to His heart and to the faith required to defeat the devil and his junk your whole life.

Do an internet search of God's love for you and read all the verses in the Bible that talk about His how special you are to Him.

Ephesians 3:17-19

And I pray that you, being rooted and established in love, may have power…to grasp how wide and long and high and deep is the love of Christ, and to know this love that surpasses knowledge—that you may be filled to the measure of all the fullness of God.

Becoming a Christian

Romans 5:8

But God demonstrates his own love for us in this: While we were still sinners, Christ died for us.

John 3:16-18

For God so loved the world that he gave his one and only Son, that whoever believes in him shall not perish but have eternal life. For God did not send his Son into the world to condemn the world, but to save the world through him. Whoever believes in him is not condemned, but whoever does not believe stands condemned already because he has not believed in the name of God's one and only Son.

The good news is that God loves us passionately and wants to spend now and eternity with us. He's not angry and trying to throw people in hell. On the contrary, He's doing everything He can to keep us out of hell and to love us back to His heart.

The one thing that sets Christianity apart from all other religions is that we aren't told we have to earn our way to heaven. It's a free gift!

Ephesians 2:8-9

For it is by grace you have been saved, through faith — and this not from yourselves, it is the gift of God — not by works, so that no one can boast.

We can't earn salvation through good deeds, going to church or by crawling ten miles on our knees to show how sorry we are. Jesus said to believe in Him and receive by faith the forgiveness and grace He earned for us when He died on the cross for our sins.

We don't become righteous in God's sight by following certain rules or laws. We become righteous and holy in God's sight when we put our faith in Jesus and believe Him implicitly, trusting Him with our lives and allowing Him to fill us with His Spirit.

Romans 3:22

This righteousness from God comes through faith in Jesus Christ to all who believe.

Salvation is a gift and must be received as a gift.

Romans 6:23

For the wages of sin is death, but the gift of God is eternal life in Christ Jesus our Lord.

When we receive Jesus and His gift of forgiveness, we choose to repent (or turn) from going our way and we choose to go God's way and follow His wisdom. We say *YES* to God in everything we do, trusting He loves us and knows what is best for us. Here are a few more verses:

John 3:35-36

The Father loves the Son and has placed everything in his hands. Whoever believes in the Son has eternal life, but whoever rejects the Son will not see life, for God's wrath remains on him.

Romans 10:9-10

If you confess with your mouth, "Jesus is Lord," and believe in your heart that God raised him from the dead, you will be saved. For it is with your heart that you believe and are justified, and it is with your mouth that you confess and are saved.

Romans 10:11-13

As the Scripture says, "Anyone who trusts in him will never be put to shame." For there is no difference between Jew and Gentile [non-Jews]—the same Lord is Lord of all and richly blesses all who call on him, for, "Everyone who calls on the name of the Lord will be saved."

If you want to receive Jesus and be forgiven of all your sins:

❖ Quit trusting in your good deeds and believe that God sent His Son into the world to forgive and save the world

❖ Call on Jesus and receive His forgiveness for your past, present and future sins

❖ Invite God's Spirit to live inside you and baptize (fill) you with His power and love

Now that you are a Believer in Jesus—a Christian:

- ❖ Find other Bible-believing Christians who can help you grow.

- ❖ Get a Bible and begin reading it daily if possible (the New Testament is a great place to start, but it's all awesome).

- ❖ Begin going to a good church that teaches you to live like Jesus and do the works Jesus said you would do because you have the Holy Spirit's power within you.

- ❖ Read or re-read the last three chapters of this book because falling in love with Jesus, falling in love with people and knowing who you are in Christ are all important keys to an amazing life as a Christian.

- ❖ Please contact Crazy About You Ministries and we can direct you to other resources to help you grow in your relationship with God. You've always been extremely loved, but now that you are God's child, He can really bless you and help you in all you do as you say *yes* to Him!

John 1:12

Yet to all who received him, to those who believed in his name, he gave the right to become children of God—

You are now a child of God. Congratulations!

God—Three-in-One

God is so incredible that He is Three yet One all at the same time—the Father, Son and Holy Spirit. This concept is somewhat similar to how each person has three parts—a body, soul (or mind) and spirit. When Jesus was being baptized by John, we saw an example of the Father, Son and Holy Spirit all operating in their separate functions at the same time. Jesus was in a body being baptized; the Holy Spirit (God's Spirit) came down in the form of a dove and rested on Jesus; and the Father spoke from heaven and said this was His beloved Son in whom He was well-pleased (see Matthew 3:16-17).

Here are some of their functions:

* ❖ The Father is running Command Central in heaven directing the angels and constantly working to love everyone and open our eyes to the truth of who He is and all that He wants to give us.

* ❖ Jesus came to earth as a man to take our punishment on Himself, but He now sits at the right hand of the Father. Jesus is interceding on our behalf because He stood in the gap between us and the Father by taking our punishment on Himself. Jesus is also doing all that the Father is doing because they are One.

* ❖ The Holy Spirit, also called God's Spirit or the Spirit of Jesus, is God with us. When someone believes in Jesus and receives His forgiveness, God's Spirit comes to live in them. A believer becomes a temple or a dwelling place for God's Spirit, and when He comes, He brings His power, love and gifts with Him.

Jesus often mentioned being One with the Father and the Spirit. In Matthew 28 He makes it clear that we are saved and baptized into the name of all three, showing again that they are One.

Matthew 28:19

Therefore go and make disciples of all nations, baptizing them in the name of the Father and of the Son and of the Holy Spirit.

The Gifts of the Spirit

I mention the gifts God's Spirit gives in chapters 1 and 4. Another great resource for those who still struggle with believing that the gifts are available for all believers is the appendix of Doug Banister's book *The Word and Power Church.*[9] He gives a biblical, thorough and loving explanation of the gifts working in us today.

Christ is the same yesterday, today and forever (Hebrews 13:8), so if Christ is unchanging, then His Spirit is unchanging. The fruit (love, joy, peace, patience) and the gifts (prophecy, healing, miracles, tongues) that were a result of His presence in a believer in Bible times will be the result of His presence in a believer today. It is the same unchanging Holy Spirit, so the effects of His presence in our lives will be unchanging. The only hindrance, both then and now, is a lack of faith or an unwillingness to receive the fruit or gifts of the Spirit.

Here are several verses on the Gifts of the Spirit, but feel free to go to biblehub.com or biblegateway.com and do a search on the Holy Spirit or on the different gifts such as healing and prophecy.

The last thing Jesus mentioned before returning to heaven was the Holy Spirit. Jesus said in Acts 1:8:

> *But you will receive power when the Holy Spirit comes on you; and you will be my witnesses in Jerusalem, and in all Judea and Samaria, and to the ends of the earth.*

Jesus was talking to all believers about receiving the power of the Holy Spirit, not just the twelve disciples. We know this because there is no way the disciples would have been able to go to the ends of the earth—to every part of the earth. That would be extremely hard for twelve people to do in our day of cars and airplanes, but completely impossible in their day of walking, horses and boats. This means Jesus was telling all believers that we will receive power when the Holy Spirit comes on us.

Acts 2:38-39

Peter replied, "Repent [turn] and be baptized, every one of you, in the name of Jesus Christ for the forgiveness of your sins. And you will receive the gift of the Holy Spirit. The promise is for you and your children and for all who are far off—for all whom the Lord our God will call."

The Holy Spirit is for all of us! If you have received Jesus, but you're not sure you've opened your heart for the Holy Spirit to baptize you in His love and power, simply invite Him to fill you to overflowing.

Acts 8:15-17

When they [Peter and John] arrived, they prayed for them that they might receive the Holy Spirit, because the Holy Spirit had not yet come upon any of them; they had simply been baptized into the name of the Lord Jesus. Then Peter and John placed their hands on them, and they received the Holy Spirit.

Once you receive the Holy Spirit, what does He promise to do through you in order to display His power?

- ❖ Love (Galatians 5:22-23)
- ❖ Speak through prophecy (1 Cor. 12:7-11)
- ❖ Heal the sick (Mark 6:18)
- ❖ Perform miracles (Acts 8:13)
- ❖ Cast out demons (Acts 8:4-8)
- ❖ Raise the dead (Matthew 10:8)
- ❖ Pray through you in a prayer language (1 Cor. 12:27-28)
- ❖ And so much more

These gifts are for you to pass out wherever you go. They are meant to strengthen, encourage and comfort those who receive them.

Paul knew the power of sharing these gifts of the Spirit. He said in his letter in Romans 1:11: *"I long to see you so that I may impart to you some spiritual gift to make you strong—"*

You and I have this same privilege of imparting spiritual gifts to strengthen and draw people to the Lord until Jesus comes back for His church—so have fun!

My Thanks

To God:
We did it! You prompted me to start this book three years ago because You knew how many challenges I would face that would slow down its progress. Your wisdom is incredible. Thank You for loving me perfectly and completely, and for being my best friend and greatest encourager. I love You more than words can express!

To Ron:
Thank you for your support and for allowing me to follow God's leading even though you and I are so different. God knew we needed each other and that together we could accomplish so much more than alone. I'm grateful we stuck it out during the painful times until we fell more in love with Jesus and grew in our ability to love each other. It's a blessing to be your wife and I'm excited to see what the future holds for us.

To My Children:
Richelle, thank you for finding time to help me with this project and for sharing your words of encouragement just when I needed them. You, Luke and Ryder are such a blessing to my heart and always bring a smile to my lips.

Dane, I'm so grateful God led you to live with us while working on your college degree. You've been one of my strongest supporters, reminding me often that I can hear God and to keep pressing forward. Thank you for expressing God's heart to me and your world.

Sierra, you were a gift to our family and we wouldn't be who we are today without you. I believe that very soon you will discover the wonder of allowing Jesus to lead you in the dance. You are His treasure and ours.

To My Parents:

Mom and Dad, you pointed me to Jesus' arms of love, and I can't thank you enough for that gift. Your lives are a sweet expression of God's heart, and you have always been there for all of your children. I love you ever for never! (My childhood version of "forever and ever.")

"Dan" Dad and Bobbie, I'm so glad we have been able to grow closer through the years. You are both special to me and I pray often that God will continue to amaze you with His love for you. Thank you for all your support and kindness. I love you.

To My Siblings:

The three I grew up with ~
Chris, your growing love for Jesus is an inspiration.
Dan, your work ethic is incredible and you make us all chuckle.
Mike, you're a terrific father and husband, and a special *little* bro.

The two I didn't live with, but got to visit ~
Lisa, I'm so glad the Lord gave me a sister. Thanks for the giggles.
Ed, you have the gift of humor and I wish we saw each other more.

I love each of you tremendously, and pray God's love will permeate your lives and thrill your hearts more and more each day!

To My Family, Friends and Former Students:

Thank you to all my wonderful family members, in-laws, dear friends and former students (Servant Evangelists, World Changers, M.Ar.C.H. co-op classes and others). It is a privilege to be a small part of each of your lives. You are incredibly loved by Jesus and me, and I know He has many exciting adventures still in store for you as you continue to say *Yes* to His loving will!

I'd like to say a special thank-you to those family and friends who supported and encouraged me as I wrote this book. You were a blessing!

Brenna Stull and Barbara Shippy:
What a gift you two have been during the past three years as we edited each other's work and cheered each other on in our writers' group. You believed in this project from the start and have stuck with me until the end. You are amazing women of God! Thank you from the bottom of my heart.

Other Editing Help:
Thank you to my friends and family who helped me edit parts of this book or who read it and shared words of encouragement. I'm afraid I'll forget a few, but thank you to each and every one: Mary Ann Earl, Kathleen Ruble, Amy Hayes, Vicki Rice, Sarah Anderson, Suzanne Taylor, Dana Eldridge, Cheri Scholz, Karis Johnston, Nancy Reed, Debbie Shea, Beckey Cortines, Donna Pfister, Matt Weiler, Randall Karcher, Scott Sullivan, Nicole Williamson, Scott and Denise Shepard and many of the family members I mentioned above.

To My Photographer and Artist:
Shig Katada, thank you for your humor, support and fantastic photography. I'll recommend Katada Kreations to everyone I know.

Eric Nishimoto, thank you for drawing my little person and for the hours you spent with the cover layout. I appreciate your kind help.

To My Endorsers and Story Contributors:
Thank you for taking time out of your busy lives and ministries to endorse or contribute a story for *No More No*. It means a great deal to me. It's exciting to see how God is using each of you powerfully!

To My Grandchildren and Future Grandchildren:
I picked the name *Lovie* for my grandma name because love is the most important thing in life—loving God, receiving God's love and loving others. Ryder, you are the only grandchild born so far, but there are two more on the way and possibly more in the future. I pray you all come to love Jesus with all your heart because He really, really loves you. (And so do I!)

Index of Stories

Growth and Inspiration (and Endnotes)

I hope you make time to watch videos, read books and check out the websites of the people and their ministries that I mentioned throughout the book and have referenced below. You'll be blessed and inspired!

---

[1]**Ann Kiemel Anderson**—Look for Ann's books such as *I'm Out to Change My World* and you'll be inspired by her love and boldness.

(1974. Reprint. Clovis: Heritage Builders, 2009. Print.)

[2] **Christ for the Nations Institute**—CFNI.org and CFN.org

[3]**Joni Eareckson Tada**—JoniandFriends.org. Joni's book entitled *Joni* inspired me to press in to Jesus no matter how hard things get.

(Tada, Joni Eareckson and Joe Musser. 1976, 1996. Reprint. Grand Rapids: Zondervan, 2001)

[4]**Bill Johnson**—BJM.org and iBethel.org. Bill's book *When Heaven Invades Earth* inspired me to begin listening for God's voice wherever I go. His many books and his teachings on YouTube and on their website will draw you closer to Jesus and reveal God's love.

(Shippensburg: Destiny Image, 2003)

[5]**Dr. James Dobson**—DrJamesDobson.org. *The Strong Willed Child* encouraged me to not give up with loving and consistent discipline.

Here is information on the latest version. (Dobson, James. *The New Strong Willed Child.* Carol Stream: Tyndale, 2004)

[6]**Heidi Baker**—IrisGlobal.org. Heidi has incredible books about God's love, miracles and supernatural provision with her orphans in Africa.

[7]**Sandra Kennedy**—SandraKennedy.org. Sandra is an excellent teacher with awesome healing stories. She has seen many miracles and has even seen people come back to life.

[8]**Dr. Douglas Banister**—*The Word and Power Church* will help you grow in your understanding of the gifts of the Spirit.
(Grand Rapids: Zondervan, 1999)

[9]**Jack Deere**—*Surprised by the Power of the Spirit* gives convincing evidence that God's Spirit and His gifts to the church are still working powerfully if we simply believe and step out by faith.
(Grand Rapids: Zondervan, 1993)

[10]**Mike Bickle**—MikeBickle.org. *Growing in the Prophetic* is a must read if you want to hear God's voice and share God's words in love and wisdom.
(1996. Reprint. Lake Mary: Charisma House, 2008. Print.)

[11]**Todd White**—LifestyleChristianity.com. Todd has powerful teachings and testimonies of healings on YouTube and on his website. He's a radical lover of Jesus.

[12]**Dan Mohler**—NeckMinistries.com. Watch Dan's teachings on YouTube. He's filled with love and walks in God's healing power.

[13]**Mark Virkler**—CWGMinistries.org. *4 Keys to Hearing God's Voice* shows that listening to God is not New Age, but biblical and vital to an intimate relationship with Jesus. Mark gives great tips for writing down what you hear. (I especially love the DVDs.)
(Shippensburg: Destiny Image, 2010)

[14]**Akiane**—Akiane.com. Akiane saw a vision of Jesus and painted it when she was eight years old (Prince of Peace). Colton Burpo, who was taken to heaven at age four, confirmed that the drawing looked like Jesus. This is how I like to picture Jesus—but smiling.

[15]**Colton Burpo**—HeavenLive.org. *Heaven is for Real* is a powerful book that gives us a peek into heaven and doesn't conflict with the biblical accounts of heaven.

(Burpo, Todd and Lynn Vincent. Nashville: Thomas Nelson, 2010)

[16]**Andrew Wommack**—AWMI.net. Andrew's teachings and the documented healing testimonies on his website will help your faith grow so that you will begin to do what Jesus said you would do.

[17]**Duane Sheriff**—DSheriff.org. Duane's free teachings on CD are packed with scriptures and incredible insights, and they're delivered with humor and warmth. He has teachings on healing, faith, hearing God's voice and much more.

Other Authors to Read

All three of these authors are connected to Bethel Church in Redding, CA and they have fantastic books on supernatural evangelism, taking risks and hearing God's voice:

Kris Vallotton
Chris Overstreet
Kevin Dedmon

Made in the USA
Charleston, SC
21 August 2015